These scriptures tc
Bible verses to reac
day devotional, thanks to my friend Pastor Eddie Cox. The reading always seems to be something I can use in my life to reflect on as I walk through life with Jesus! Praise God! Amen!

Russell Theobalt

I am so thankful for the daily devotionals that I receive from Pastor Eddie Cox. So many days I feel like God is speaking directly to me through Eddie's words, and other days I know exactly who I need to share the devotion with. Eddie's love for God shines through his words and opens my eyes to God's grace, glory, and love for all. I'm embarrassed to admit that some days I am so busy that I fail to put God first, and the daily verse that I receive from Pastor Cox draws me back and reminds me that God's love is always with me and that He wants me to be a blessing to someone else. I can't thank Eddie enough for sharing his love for God with me and so many others. He is an amazing blessing.

Rachel Lehman

So many daily devotionals are inspirational, feel-good messages that start folks' day off positively in a milky fashion. Pastor Eddie has brought me God's Word with the same positivity and so much more. I have been refreshed, motivated, and have a feel-good walk away; however, these are so much more. I walk away convicted, inspired, and thought-provoked. I have been fed an adult portion of God's message brought to us through His servant Pastor Eddie Cox. Thank you for sharing what He had given to you. Your blessings flow through you. Someone shout GLORY, and may it be all to God.

William Freeman

Thank you for these devotionals that are inspirational and sustaining. They bring me peace and closeness to our Lord as reminders to place my trust in Him to alleviate my fears and worries. I feel His presence with these devotionals. He is the way of life!

Minnie Capella

I find these devotionals to really bring the Word of God alive. Eddie takes the Scriptures and then talks about how God's Word applies to our lives and situations. His ending prayer really brings it all together as we pray for God's guidance. Eddie is truly the "hands and feet of Jesus."

Donna Irwin

I look forward with anticipation to the scripture, life application, and prayer that Eddie shares each day. Two and half years ago, I was diagnosed with Stage 4 pancreatic cancer. I consider myself a survivor because of many praying warriors and a plan that God had for me that was far better than I ever imagined. I have needed the daily reassurance of God's love for me, the power of His healing, and His words of protection, strength, unconditional love, and grace. Eddie's devotionals have supplied all these things and more. The devotionals are a reminder that no matter what I'm going through I'm not walking alone because God is always with me. Thank you, Eddie!

Jan Nelson

Glory! Of all the big stories about Jesus in the Bible—the feeding of the five thousand, the Sermon on the Mount—it is the one-on-one encounters that mean the most to me. Jesus at the well, Jesus on the road to Emmaus, Jesus with Peter on the beach. Eddie Cox lives his big life— with God and with his fellow man—one person at a time. Intentional intimacy is more than a name. It is a call to genuine praise and testimony. Thanks, pastor.

Rick Morgan

These devotions immensely bless me and provide a spiritual spark to my mornings. The verses, Spirit-led word, and prayer that Eddie shares continually speak to what I have going on during that time and allow me to hear God's voice loud and clear. I can hardly wait for each morning's devotion. They have made a huge impact in my life and the fifty-plus people I share them with each day!

Steven Wilkerson

How many of us just go through the day not realizing how special to God that we are? Have you ever felt like why would God love me or why would God pay attention to me? This is the heart of Intentional Intimacy Ministries, reminding God's people of the plan, purpose, and promise of God's love and goodwill toward His creation. That is what those daily devotions have meant to me. Life quickly gets so busy that I find myself at times in autopilot mode, and what this ministry continues to remind me is that I am called to be intentional with my time, I am commanded to have a deep intimate relationship with my God and His people, and in doing so, I find myself doing the very thing that God calls us all to do: ministry.

Keanan Bovie

Conversations with God

100 Devotions to Transform Your Heart, Mind and Soul

BY EDDIE COX

Conversations with God: 100 Devotions to Transform Your Heart, Mind and Soul

Published by Intentional Intimacy Ministries, 3838 Oak Lawn Ave., Suite 1500, Dallas, Texas, 75219-4516

ISBN
Paperback 979-8-9873983-0-2
eBook 979-8-9873983-1-9

Book Cover Design by BluDesign.com, Nashville, TN
Text Design by YouPublish (youpublish.com)
www.intentionalintimacyministries.com

Printed in the United States of America

CONTENTS

FOREWORD

On a scale of one to ten, how would you rate your prayer life?

If yours is a ten, you may not need this book. You may already be wearing holes in the knees of your pants from a regular, continuous, meaningful conversation with God on behalf of yourself, your family, your church, and your community.

This book is for the rest of us.

I can vividly recall the day I met Pastor Eddie Cox. Actually, you don't meet Eddie, you encounter him. I had traveled for twenty years with a career in technology consulting. God then steered me to the Cornerstone Heights neighborhood in South Dallas, one of Dallas' poorest, where Eddie was hard at work ministering to formerly incarcerated, homeless, and addicted men at a faith-based ministry, the Men of Nehemiah. When I walked through the door, Eddie was one of the first people I met, and he was unexpected.

I was amazed at the level of poverty in Cornerstone Heights. While I was generally aware of the conditions, I had never spent significant time surrounded by it. I learned that the root cause of poverty is the inability to maintain productive relationships. The psalmist says we are all fearfully and wonderfully made, but it's easier to believe that you're not, that you have nothing to offer. For the people whom Eddie Cox ministers to, relationships with family and friends, along with most forms of support, have long since lapsed. Poor physical health and mental issues, coupled with substance abuse, make basic communication difficult. Without communication, there is no relationship. Changing this multigenerational culture is too hard.

This was my theory, until I encountered Eddie Cox.

William Carey said, "Expect great things from God; attempt great things for God," and never had I experienced greater things being attempted and achieved than watching Eddie impact the lives of men and women in Cornerstone Heights. Eddie walked his talk, and that's how I define integrity. I never heard Eddie say he was too tired, or too busy, or too absorbed with his own life challenges or short on resources. He provided physical, mental, and spiritual support without expecting gratitude. In Cornerstone Heights, gratitude is difficult, because life is difficult. The only resource Eddie needed was the Bible.

The Bible is a book about relationships, and we are instructed to use prayer to enter into a conversation with God. We know prayer is certainly a two-way conversation, yet one of the most common mistakes we make is forgetting to give God time to speak. What we have in this book is Eddie telling us how God speaks to him.

Jeremiah 3:15 says, "And I will give you pastors according to mine heart, which shall feed you with knowledge and understanding" (KJV). Far greater than preaching are the kindness, compassion, and love that radiate from the life of a pastor. People will soon forget a sermon no matter how good it is, but they will never forget the impact of a pastor who has been with them during the difficult times in their lives. That indelible impact, created from relationships that many felt were not possible, is where Eddie has made his mark—all because he listened to God.

As your heart is moved by years of prayer compiled in this book by Pastor Eddie Cox, make a new resolution today: you are going to make your whole life a prayer, and you will devote some amount of time each day in conversation with God. He's waiting to hear from you. And He's waiting to pour out His blessings in return.

Jim Ramsey
Principal, Visorie Consulting

ACKNOWLEDGEMENTS

I would like to thank Rick Morgan for his love for God and God's people and the desire to see these daily devotionals in book form. I want to thank the Board of Intentional Intimacy Ministries, Steven, Keanan, Rick for your love and support. I want to thank Bruce Barbour of Literary Management Group for your insight and help in publishing this book of devotions. I want to thank my family, kids, grandkids, and many friends for their unfailing love. I want to thank all those who are growing and will start a journey of growing in an intentional intimate relationship with God through these devotions.

INTRODUCTION

As you read these devotions allow the Holy Spirit to open your heart, mind, and soul to growing into an intentional intimacy with God. This is the first step in building an intimate relationship with the Father, with the Son, and the Holy Spirit. This can be accomplished as you journey in prayer, studying the Scriptures and sharing your faith.

As you come with a Spirit of longing and a desire to know God intimately, it will stir up an insatiable desire to know God in the fullness of His revelation. With joyful expectation, let us prepare our heart to receive revelation, inspiration, and authentication from the Word of God.

The world is too much among us; we need to learn how to shake it off and come before the presence of the Almighty God. Let us surrender and consecrate ourselves to God and allow our heart, mind, and soul to get in a submissive and obedient position to hear God speak.

There is an old hymn by Charles Albert Tindley, "Nothing Between My Soul and the Savior," that when read or sung can put you in position to receive God's revelation and hear Him speak.

> Nothing between my soul and the Savior,
> Naught of this world's delusive dream:

> I have renounced all sinful pleasure:
> Jesus is mine, there's nothing between.
>
> Nothing between my soul and the Savior,
> So that His blessed face may be seen:
> Nothing preventing the least of His Favor,
> Keep the way clear! Let nothing between.
>
> Nothing between, likely world pleasure:
> Habits of life, Though harmless they seem,
> Must my heart from Him e'er sever:
> He is my all, there's nothing between.
>
> Nothing between, like pride or station:
> Self-life or friends shall not intervene:
> Though it may cost me tribulation,
> I am resolved: there's nothing between.
>
> Nothing between, e'en many hard trials,
> Though the whole world against me convene:
> Watching with prayer and much self-denial,
> I'll triumph at last, with nothing between.

As you embark on the pursuit of an intentional intimacy with God, let A. W. Tozer's words be an encouragement to you: "The cost is certainly high. The pathway rough. The way forward is often lonely. But the rewards you will gain of knowing God in intimate fellowship will be well worth the journey."

Eddie Cox, President
Intentional Intimacy Ministries

ANSWERED PRAYER

Dear friends, if our hearts do not condemn us, we have confidence before God and receive from him anything we ask, because we keep his commands and do what pleases him. And this is his command: to believe in the name of his Son, Jesus Christ, and to love one another as he commanded us.

1 John 3:21–23, NIV

The Bible says God has laid out five conditions to answered prayer: we have an honest relationship with Him, we harbor no unforgiveness toward anyone, we're willing to share the results with other people, we ask Him in faith, and we pray in Jesus' name.

Have we been overlooking any of these conditions? Maybe we've been holding a grudge. Maybe we've been nursing resentment and we've allowed bitterness to build up in our life. Maybe we've been refusing to admit some wrong in our life. We have known it was there, but we haven't wanted to go to Him and say: "You're right, God; that's wrong. I admit it."

Maybe we've prayed, but we've never really expected God to answer. If we don't expect God to answer, we're just wasting our time. Or maybe we haven't been abiding in God's Word and growing in faith. Maybe we haven't been willing to share God's blessings with other people.

We've been hesitant to give back to God a percentage of all the things He has blessed us with. When our heart is lined up with the Word of God and aligned to the will of God, we will indeed receive what we ask, because our petition will be a correct and godly request that is pleasing in His sight.

Being aligned to the Word and the will of God ensures that we who are walking in spirit and truth will pray as led by the Holy Spirit, and our prayer will indeed be answered!!!

Father, thank You for this day, and thank You for the privilege of prayer, and that through Christ we have access to the throne of grace. Lord, let Your abundant blessings flow like a mighty river over us and our family today. Lord, thank You that You hear and answer the prayers and intercessions of Your children that are aligned to Your will and the Word of truth. Lord, we pray that the thoughts and the petition of our hearts may remain in accordance with Your perfect purpose and plan, and we pray that You would guide us into all truth so that our life may be pleasing in Your sight. Lord, use us to be a bold witness of Your mercy and grace to those who need it today.

Father, we love You. Amen.

NOTES

MATURITY AND SANCTIFICATION

Now may the God of peace Himself sanctify you completely; and may your whole spirit, soul, and body be preserved blameless at the coming our Lord Jesus Christ. He who calls you is faithful, who also will do it.

1 Thessalonians 5:23–24, NKJV

Full maturity and the complete sanctification of each and every believer's spirit, soul, and body are these scriptures' earnest desires for all Christians. Some incorrectly consider that we can reach sinless perfection in this life, but this is unbiblical, for our old sin nature, which resides within our mortal bodies, lusts against our new life in Christ, and this will continue until we discard this fallen, earthy, mortal frame and are taken to be with the Lord forever.

We are set apart for the Lord, or positionally sanctified, the moment that we place our faith in the Lord Jesus. But for the rest of our lives, we are being progressively sanctified as we mature in the faith and grow in grace while submitting to the ongoing work of the Holy Spirit within our lives.

Scripture tells us that our complete and final sanctification will only be attained when we take up our eternal position in heaven, when through death or the rapture we will reach full and perfect sanctification, when the God of peace Himself sanctifies us entirely and our whole spirit and soul and body will be preserved complete and without blame at the coming of our Lord Jesus Christ.

What a glorious promise. May today we walk worthy of our calling and look to Jesus, the Author and Finisher of our salvation, in spirit, soul, and body!!!

Father, thank You for this day and Your amazing mercy and grace. Lord, let Your abundant blessings be our family's portion today. Lord, give us Your mind so that our body may be a temple of the spirit of holiness that is Yours. Lord, may Yourself make us holy through and through. Lord, may our spirit, soul, and body be kept blameless by your power. Lord, we trust You to do this because You are the one who has called us, and You are faithful. Lord, we ask for growth in Your amazing grace today. Lord, use us to be the light of Your love to those who You bring Your way today.

Father, we love You. Amen.

NOTES

SPIRITUAL CONSISTENCY

Be alert and of sober mind. Your enemy the devil prowls around like a roaring lion looking for someone to devour. Resist him, standing firm in the faith, because you know that the family of believers throughout the world is undergoing the same kind of sufferings. And the God of all grace, who called you to his eternal glory in Christ, after you have suffered a little while, will himself restore you and make you strong, firm and steadfast. To him be the power forever and ever. Amen.

1 Peter 5:8–11, NIV

Every serious-minded child of God identifies with Peter's struggle for spiritual consistency. Bold to declare his allegiance to Jesus, Peter was also quick to sell out his commitment under pressure. Paul describes our dilemma: "Although I want to do good, evil is right there with me." The truth is that where the Lord works, Satan "prowls around like a roaring lion looking for someone to devour." Jesus announces free forgiveness, yet Satan makes us question whether we are worth saving.

When truth is declared, Satan questions the Bible's reliability. Satan is committed to derailing God's work. So we are called to "be alert and of sober mind." How? First of all, we need to learn God's truth. We must accept God's Word, take it into our hearts, and obey its commands. We must also listen to advice.

By seeking the guidance of trusted seasoned believers, we learn from the experience of others and tap into their God-given wisdom and insight. Also, we must live in prayer. We daily humble ourselves before God, confessing our sins and seeking His guidance. Satan is on the prowl. Now even the most vigilant among us are going to stub their toe once in a while because we are human, therefore sinners, and fall short of the glory of God.

Therefore, we can take comfort in knowing that all of our brothers and sisters in Christ have similar experiences and suffer at one time or another from failure to stay on watch at all times. Even though we will all fall short at one time or another throughout our life, it is important to heed Peter's words and always try to "be sober-minded; be watchful"(1 Pet. 5:8, ESV). Our next fall could be closer than we think. But we need not fear. God's grace equips us to be vigilant and to stand firm in Jesus!!!

Father, thank You for this day and waking us up and setting us on our journey through it. Lord, open the storehouses of heaven and pour out Your abundant blessings upon us and our family today. Lord, we know we are Your children but are often assaulted by the evil one. Lord, protect us from temptation and write Your truth on our hearts. Lord, make us more aware of the schemes of your enemy. Lord, we invite You to grant us the faith to resist and for the courage to place all our hope in You. Lord, use us to love others as You love them.

Father, we love You. Amen.

NOTES

FULL AND ABSOLUTE DEVOTION TO GOD

And they were calling to one another: "Holy, holy, holy is the Lord *Almighty; the whole earth is full of his glory."*

Isaiah 6:3, NIV

Then I heard the voice of the Lord saying, "Whom shall I send? And who will go for us?" And I said, "Here am I. Send me!"

Isaiah 6:8, NIV

Throughout Scripture we see a powerful principle exemplified: when God is seen for who He truly is, the natural response of the seer is full and absolute devotion. When God reveals His glory, love, power, holiness, and splendor, the seer responds with absolute commitment and worship.

I believe that God would reveal Himself to us today in simple but mighty ways. I believe that He longs for us to see Him as He truly is, and that His chief desire is our devotion. May we see God face-to-face today and be forever changed by a fresh revelation of this God who would give up everything for a relationship with us.

Isaiah 6 exemplifies both a vison of God and a response of devotion. Isaiah has an open vision of the majesty of God in heaven. He sees God on his throne and hears angels declaring

His holiness and splendor by saying: "Holy, holy, holy is the LORD of hosts; the whole earth is full of his glory!" (v. 3, ESV). And in response to this vision, Isaiah 6:8 says: "Then I heard the voice of the Lord saying, 'Whom shall I send, and who will go for us?' Then I said: 'Here I am! Send me.'" Isaiah responds to seeing God with full devotion. God doesn't ask for our devotion the way man does. He doesn't offer us ultimatums or transactionally based benefits if we will love Him.

Devotion to Him is meant to be the natural response of seeing God for who He is, because He is inherently worthy of every bit of devotion we can bring to Him. He is worthy of our allegiance because He is the King of Kings. He is worthy of our obedience because His will is both knowable and perfect. He is worthy of our worship because He is the almighty God to whom all creation offers ceaseless praise. And He is worthy of our heart because He is the God of love and mercy who has created us for relationship with Him.

Too often we mistake God's mercy and grace as opportunities to go our own way and come back to Him as we please or when we need something. Too often we treat His love as an opiate for our problems rather than the foundation on which we devote our lives in humble submission to Him. God is patient. He is kind. He will never force or manipulate us into loving Him. But His patience, kindness, and gentleness do not change the fact that He is King of kings, Lord of lords, and Creator of all, and that He is worthy and deserving of our ceaseless devotion. Run to meet your God in the secret place today.

Look upon His face and see Him for both the loving and majestic God He is. He longs to reveal His nature to us. He longs for us to search out the depths of Him and be awed by His wonder and mystery. Spend time in prayer meeting with your loving heavenly Father and responding to His nature with our love, worship, and devotion.

Father, thank You for this day and the praise in our hearts for You and Your Son. Lord, open the windows of heaven and shine down Your abundant blessings over us and our family today. Holy God, Holy Father, Holy King of the ages, we praise You for the wonderful gift of Your grace. Lord, You have made us worthy and holy by your sacrificial blood. Lord, may we truly enter to worship and depart to serve, saying, "Lord, here we are, send us! Lord, use us to share Your gospel of life and grace to all we meet today.

Father, we love You. Amen.

NOTES

RICH INHERITANCE AS A CHILD OF GOD

The Spirit Himself bears witness with our spirit that we are children of God, and if children, then heirs—heirs of God and joint heirs with Christ, if indeed we suffer with Him, that we may also be glorified together.

Romans 8:16–17, NKJV

As long as we are born again, we are no longer a "slave," but a child of the Most High God. And God does not just call us His child, He also calls us "an heir" through Christ. In fact, the Word says that you are "joint heirs" with Christ. As a joint heir with Christ Jesus, we inherit everything that He is. How precious Jesus is to the Father is how precious we are to the Father. The way the Father loves Jesus is the way the Father loves us! How accepted are we by God today?

Look at Jesus. That is how accepted we are! Christ is the measure of our acceptance. How favored are we by God? Look at Jesus, who is seated at the Father's right hand. We enjoy that same favor today because whatever Christ enjoys, we enjoy! As a joint heir with Christ Jesus, we also inherit all that He has obtained from the Father. How much Jesus has is how much we have. I used to read the Bible to find out how to be a successful and victorious Christian. But now, I read it to find out more about Jesus because I know that when I find Him, I find my every blessing in Him. All that Jesus is in heaven today, we are in this world. All that belongs to Him belongs to us.

That is why it is in your interest to know Him more, to see Him in all His glory and beauty. And because Jesus is so glorious, it will take you a lifetime to discover everything that He has done for us and has for us. Friends, we are an heir of the Most High God. We are a joint heir with Christ Jesus. So find out all the blessings that our rich inheritance includes through His Word and our relationship with Him, and start walking in them today!!!

Father, we thank You for this day and our identity we have in Jesus. Lord, open the floodgates of heaven and pour out Your abundant blessings upon us and our family today. Lord, we ask You to help us to understand these scriptures today. Lord, we thank You for the work of the Spirit in our lives. Lord, what a wonderful thing it is that You have called us to be children of the living God. Lord, help us never to forget it, and to walk worthy of such a calling. Lord, use us to be the touch of Your love to someone who needs it today.

Father, we love You. Amen.

NOTES ______________________________

SPIRITUAL WARRIOR

Blessed be the Lord *my Rock, who trains my hands for war, and my fingers for battle—my loving kindness and my fortress, my high tower and my deliverer, my shield and the One in whom I take refuge, who subdues my people under me.*

Psalm 144:1–2, NKJV

Happy are the people who are in such a state; happy are the people whose God is the Lord*!*

Psalm 144:15, NKJV

Do you ever feel like you're in the middle of a war? The Christian life isn't always a warm and fuzzy experience. Sometimes we find ourselves in a spiritual battle. It's easy to feel vulnerable and exposed at these times.

We must remember, however, we are not fighting these battles in our own strength. In today's passage, King David praised the Lord, recognizing that it was God who had enabled him to win the victory over his enemies. Moreover, the Lord had taught him how to fight and protected him. What does God's boot camp entail? How does He train us for war? The term "trains" here refers to an exercise in learning.

Here's a nugget of truth from the passage: we may not know why we're in a battle, but we can be sure God wants to teach us something. He's walking us through an exercise in learning. Don't let the battle shake us from our firm foundation in Christ. Remember, the Lord is our rock. The Hebrew word for "rock" used here is *tsur*. It highlights God's stability and the protection that He supplies whenever we are in the battle. God's got us solidly covered. He won't hesitate or weaken from day to day.

The Lord is loving, kind, and loyal; He will provide a fortress for us in the storms of life. He is our high tower, our deliverer, our shield, and our refuge. God promises to subdue our enemies. The battle cannot be fought and won by flesh and blood alone.

In Ephesians 6:10–18, the apostle Paul outlines a six-piece set of armor, our spiritual defense against the enemy of our souls. The armor of God may be invisible, but it's just as real as military equipment. When we use it properly and wear it daily, it provides solid protection against the enemy's onslaught.

Let God train your hands for war, and you'll be supernaturally equipped with the only firepower needed against Satan's attacks. And remember, God is your protection and shield. Bless Him and praise Him! You don't have to fight the battle alone!!!

Father, thank You for this day and Your strength and authority to walk in it. Lord, let Your abundant blessings be our family's portion today. Lord, we ask for You to be our Rock and prepare our fingers, hands, and hearts for the battles that You can already see coming at us today. Lord, help us to know that You are on our side and that when times are tough, we can call on You to be our deliverer. Lord, help us to sing praises to Your holy name. Lord, help us to be happy and find joy in serving

You. Lord, use us to be a bold witness of Your mercy and grace to all that come our way.

Father, we love You. Amen.

NOTES

WHAT IS FAITH?

Now faith is the substance of things hoped for, the evidence of things not seen. For by it, the elders obtained a good testimony. By faith we understand that the worlds were framed by the word of God, so that the things which are seen were not made of things which are visible.

Hebrews 11:1–3, NKJV

This all-encompassing verse explains both what faith in Jesus Christ is and what faith does. The heart of faith develops its own eyes, which see spiritual things coming that can't yet be seen by the physical eye.

When the author, under the inspiration of the Holy Spirit, writes, "Faith is the substance," he uses a single Greek word *hupostasis*, meaning "to stay under, a foundation." So faith is the foundation on which all our hopes for the future are built. Faith doesn't make imaginary things come true, but rather it enables God's people to live with certainty and confidence in the realities that are true, though not yet physically visible.

Mature believers who have trusted God through years of great trials, sorrow, and pain will tell us that Jesus has become so real and precious to them that they are absolutely confident of His promises. When we choose to look with eyes of faith, we become more and more confident of the reality of God and what awaits us in eternity. And as we are commanded to love others, we are compelled to share the truth we have found in Jesus with those around us.

Many will not appreciate our responsibility to tell others and will complain of our freedom to express it openly. But love leaves us no other recourse than to care about others enough to share the truth of Jesus Christ's dying so they might live.

Do you want a stronger faith, a better faith, a more alive faith, a more active faith? Guess what you have to do? You need to spend time with the Word. You need to be in the Word. You need to read the Word and study the Word and meditate on the Word. You need to absorb the Word. It needs to permeate your thoughts, your feelings, your emotions, your will, your life. Do this over and over again. Because faith comes by hearing!!!

Father, thank You for this day and the measure of faith You have given us. Lord, pour out Your abundant blessings from the storehouses of heaven upon us and our family today. Lord, we thank You for the gift of faith. Lord, we thank You for raising us to spiritual life and giving us the ability to receive what You have said through Your Word. Lord, we thank You that faith is not based on nonsense but on facts, history, eyewitnesses, and good evidence. Lord, help us to present Your gospel and all things in Your Word with reasons to all those who ask today.

Father, we love You. Amen.

NOTES

NEED DIRECTION IN LIFE?

I will instruct you and teach you in the way you should go; I will guide you with My eye.

Psalm 32:8, NKJV

Need direction in life? God is willing to teach, instruct, and guide us. The promise in this verse is God's provision for those who are willing to receive Him by faith and follow His leading. Let's listen to what God says He will do if we are willing to be taught by Him and follow Him. (1) He will instruct us, (2) He will teach us in the way we should go, (3) He will counsel us with His eyes on us. It is the Lord's desire to teach us in the way in which He would have us to go through submission and obedience to His Word and His authority.

As a believer, we *must* seek and obey with humility, live in holiness, walk daily in integrity, be honest in our dealings with one another, and be faithful to God and the task that He has assigned to our hands, just to name a few. God did not save us to live life as we please.

In His Word, there is a standard of living for us Christians in which God has established for us to live by. Direction is important for without it we get lost. Many are lost today because they refuse to be taught by God and instead by self, they refuse to go the way in which God has already mapped out for us in His Word, and they refuse to be counseled by God and be guided by God's eyes. Instead, they choose to be instructed and guided by what their eyes see in the world and follow after that counsel. Man can instruct, but it is only God, through His Holy Spirit, who can make us understand truth, for God says: "if you hold to my teachings, you are really my disciples." Jn 8:31

As God continues to teach and instruct us in the way of salvation, He promises to keep a watchful eye on us. He will not leave us to ourselves for He knows without His direction and His watchful eyes upon us, like sheep, we will stray away from the path of righteousness. Looking for direction in life? Not sure about how to travel down the road of salvation after you have accepted Christ? Get in the Word of God, pray and seek the Lord's face for His promises to teach, instruct, and keep a watchful eye over us!!!

Father, thank You for Your Word that sustains us as we walk in this day. Lord, let Your abundant blessings fall upon us and our family from the windows of heaven. Lord, You are our hiding place. Lord, you are the One we seek. Lord, You are the protection we need. Lord, we yearn for Your advice, Your guidance, and Your help. Show me which way to turn. Lord, You are the victory we seek. Lord, use us to be the light of Your love to those You bring our way.

Father, we love You. Amen.

NOTES ______________________________

____

____

HEART REFLECTION

Do all things without complaining and disputing, that you may become blameless and harmless, children of God without fault in the midst of a crooked and perverse generation, among whom you shine as lights in the world, holding fast the word of life, so that I may rejoice in the day of Christ that I have not run in vain or labored in vain.

Philippians 2:14–16, NKJV

Our words reflect our hearts. The first step in combating a complaining attitude is to control what we allow our minds to focus on. This means taking every thought captive. The world is watching to see if what we say we believe is reflected in how we live our lives. Our purpose in the here and now is to reflect Christ to a world that is desperately searching for a Savior.

As we run this amazing race of life for God's glory, we have an opportunity to show the world the difference Christ makes in us through our love, actions, choices, and speech. This world will disappoint us, try to defeat us, and discourage us to no end. But we are not made for this world, and so our source of joy is not found here either.

When we view our earthy home as what it is—temporary—we are free to hold this world loosely, knowing heaven is coming. Instead of allowing complaints and arguments to waste our time, may we choose to focus our minds on ways to be a light in this world to a generation who desperately needs Jesus.

Keep in mind what Paul has just been talking about. He urged the Philippians to adopt the mindset, attitude, and stance of Jesus, the one who gave up all for the sake of love, love for us. More than that, Paul urged them to accept God's invitation to be loved, renewed, and transformed. And now he's encouraging them to remember who they are, not children of the world without hope who run after acceptance by fitting in, by doing whatever everyone else is doing simply because everyone else is doing it. Rather, they are children of God.

And so he invites them to be different because they are different—adopted and blessed by God and intended to shine like stars by their willingness to share love when the world says hold back, to work for peace when the world urges war, and to seek reconciliation when the world wants to divide everyone into sides. Be different because we are different. Be different because you are God's beloved children. Be different to make me, Paul, proud. Be different because you might inspire others to be different too. Be different, finally, because you can.

Father thank You for this day and Your amazing grace that it holds. Lord, let Your abundant blessings be our family's portion today. Lord, we thank You for calling us to be a place of light in the dark world around us, and we pledge to shine Your light today in the lives of all. Lord, remind us of who we are: Your beloved and oh so different children, created in Your image and destined to shine like stars as we share Your love for the world.

Lord, let our light shine bright and light a path to You to those who are lost in the darkness of this world.

Father, we love You. Amen.

NOTES

FEAR DISPELLED BY TRUST

Fear of man will prove to be a snare, but
whoever trusts in the Lord is kept safe.

Proverbs 24:25, NIV

Being concerned about what someone else is thinking or can do is a common fear that many people have. They are more worried about what someone may think than is necessary. When that fear is high enough, one will be trapped into doing what the other person wants. Some will make poor choices based off their fear of someone else.

The more poor choices are made, the more entangled in a web the person gets. Living like this does not bring peace or comfort. As time goes along, the snare gets tighter and tighter, destroying one's life. Solomon had recognized that one cannot fear man without getting trapped in a snare. Yet, he also knew that in order to be safe, all one had to do is trust in God. People will take advantage of those who fear them. They will make the one who fears do things that is not wanted or desired. Selfishness will rise up and cause the fear to increase in another. Ultimately, destruction will come about. Those feared will keep rising up in power, seizing what they can.

We who do not fear man but trust in God will not be trapped in the snare. We will be kept safe. God will open our eyes to see the reality that is around them. We will be able to see the snares that have been placed in front of them and walk a different path. God does not want us to walk in fear, but in trust, knowing that He is in control. The path that God leads us on is one that will build up and not destroy.

It is a path that leads them toward eternal life, rather than temporary happiness and death. There will be people in our lives at times who appear to be in control. They will appear to be the ones calling the shots in our lives. Do not fear them. They are temporary and leading down the wrong path.

Put all of your trust in God, knowing that He is in control. The things that man can do are only temporary and can do no real harm to us. We have a choice to make as to who you will fear and follow. Do you want a snare that is dangerous, or do you want life and safety?

Father, thank You for this day and for waking us up and setting us on our way. Lord, pour out your abundant blessings from the floodgates of heaven. Let them rain down over us and our family today. Lord, we choose to put our trust in You. Lord, we choose to press forward and overcome fear. Lord, we believe You have our best interest at heart and know that You are leading us in the paths of righteousness. Lord, open our eyes to the snares around us in the paths of righteousness. Lord open our eyes to the snares around us and keep us safe from any harm. Lord, use us to be a bold witness of Your gospel of saving grace to those in our path today.

Father, we love You. Amen.

NOTES ______________________________

____

THE LORD REIGNS

The LORD reigns, He is clothed with majesty; the LORD is clothed, He has girded Himself with strength. Surely the world is established, so that it cannot be moved. Your throne is established from of old; You are from everlasting.

Psalm 93:1–2, NKJV

There is one constant in life of which we can be very sure: the Lord reigns. He has reigned from eternity past and will continue to reign for eternity to come. He is the One who established this world, and without Him it cannot be moved.

Due to recent weather, we all know the power of the hurricane and the power of tsunamis, and yet the Lord is mightier than the noise of many waters and the mighty waves of the sea. That should give us a great sense of peace. In a time when the threat of terrorism, nuclear war, or a coronavirus is constantly upon us, we are reminded that man can do nothing to destroy this world that God has created.

If indeed destruction of the world comes, it will come at the hand of God due to the great sin and wickedness of mankind. What an amazing God we serve, and how wondrous and glorious that the true believer can rest safely in Him. We do not need to fear the terror by day or night, for at all times we are resting safely in His guidance and protection.

Even when the days of adversity come, we know that God sends only what we need to grow us to become more and more like Him. And He promises that when we go through the waters of adversity, He will go right along with us! Pray today that you will go about your day in peace thinking about this psalm and knowing that God reigns over everything; there is nothing that man can do against the everlasting power of God!!!

Father, thank You for this day and the breath of Your Word. Lord, open the storehouses of Your abundant blessings, and pour them upon us and our family today. Lord, we praise You for Your majesty, Your power, Your wisdom, and Your holiness. Lord, we know that we cannot really understand or fathom Your greatness or just how awesome You are, but You have revealed enough to us that we can know You are God. Lord, give us a loving heart today for those who are lost in the darkness of this world.

Father, we love You. Amen.

NOTES

GLORY IN SUFFERING

Not only so, but we also glory in our sufferings, because we know that suffering produces perseverance; perseverance, character; and character, hope. And hope does not put us to shame, because God's love has been poured out into our hearts through the Holy Spirit, who has been given to us.

Romans 5:3–5, NIV

There is no vacation from human suffering and tragedy. And a lot of people try to sort this out, understand it, and explain it. C. S. Lewis called it "the problem of pain." But there is a God who, despite the worst tragedy, can bring good out of bad. We acknowledge that life can be bad. We acknowledge that bad things can happen. We acknowledge that God is sovereign, which means that He is in control. And we acknowledge that ultimately God can cause all things to work together for good for those who love Him and are called according to His purpose.

Yet some hold the view that because they are Christians, they won't suffer. They may not state it outright, but they believe that bad things won't happen to them. However, the reality is that we will face trouble too. Jesus said, "In the world you will have tribulation; but be of good cheer, I have overcome the world" (NKJV).

We may have a hard time putting the words "trials," "problems," and "God loves me" into one sentence because they don't seem to go together. But let's take a look at God's endgame. Is it to make us happy in the temporal, or is it to prepare us for heaven? The latter is the answer. So God can allow tragedy. No tragedy is good. But God can bring good despite a tragedy.

So even in our worst of times, if we can be people of character, then nothing can steal from us our most desired goal, the character of God, given us in Jesus Christ!!!

Father, thank You for this day and the mercy and grace to walk in it. Lord, let Your abundant blessings flow over us and our family today. Lord, please help us be strong in difficult times and consistent in holy character. Lord, please give us a heart of courage and compassion. Lord, give us the strength to endure. Lord, when hard times come our way, help us to look to You for perseverance and joy. Lord, make us mature and complete through these trials. Lord, use us to be the beacon of Your love to those who need it today.

Father, we love You. Amen.

NOTES

WISE AND HARMLESS

Behold, I send you out as sheep in the midst of wolves. Therefore be wise as serpents and harmless as doves.

Matthew 10:16, NKJV

Wise as serpents and innocent as doves. I don't know about you, but that almost sounds like an oxymoron (words that we put together but are exact opposites) to me. You know, like "Pretty ugly." "A little big." "Act natural." "Adult children." "Altogether separate." But the difference here is that God is telling us to be wise as serpents and innocent as doves. He's combining the attributes. We aren't to be only wise. That can lead to pride and haughtiness. However, neither are we to be only innocent.

While innocence is definitely a needed trait in a believer, God doesn't want us to be oblivious to circumstances in our life or situations we may find ourselves in. That all being said, while so many of us emphasize and strive for the "innocent" factor in our life, when was the last time we said to ourselves, "I need to work on being wise like a serpent?" Jesus' followers will be like sheep hunted by a den of wolves.

In such circumstances, two qualities are not only essential but also commanded. Jesus' followers are to be bright, insightful, strategic, smart, clever, and wise. In other words, we won't stupidly muddle through when opposed. We do not want to bring unnecessary shame or hardship on ourselves, the cause of

Christ, or Jesus' people. Second, even if we are hounded, criticized, and despised, let's make sure we are a people of character, peace, and purity.

Clearly, the apostle Peter got the message, because a reading of 1 Peter teaches us how to practically live out what Jesus teaches here: purity and prudence in a hostile world in which we live as witnesses to Jesus Christ and His kingdom. Let this be a focus in your time of meditation throughout the day!!!

Father, thank You for this day and the breath of Your Word that sustains us. Lord, open the floodgates of heaven and rain down Your abundant blessings upon us and our family. Lord, give us wisdom to face those who despise Your name, Your cause, Your message, and Your people. Lord, create in us a pure heart that we might know You. Lord, use us to be a light in this dark and fallen world.

Father, we love You. Amen.

NOTES

TRULY THANKFUL

For everything God created is good, and nothing is to be rejected if it is received with thanksgiving, because it is consecrated by the word of God and prayer.

1 Timothy 4:4–5, NIV

God is great, God is good, let us thank Him for our food." That prayer, often spoken by small children before they eat, may seem simple, yet thankfulness is something we often struggle with even as adults.

How often have we stopped and thanked God for the air we breathe, the abilities we have, or the body we have been given? Of course, gratefulness does not just manifest itself in words but becomes part of our lives. When we truly understand the gifts that God has given us, it leads us to a desire to serve Him. Then, as we meditate on the gospel and the fact that Jesus died on our behalf so we could be forgiven, it should cause us to give our all for Him. Knowing that it can be difficult in our busy lives to stop and focus on all that we are blessed with, but when we take the time to, it will impact our lives profoundly.

As we focus on the goodness of God and His provision for our lives and our salvation, we are humbled and put in the perfect place to be used by God. Even in our times of hardship, when we stand back and view, we get a glimpse of God's eternal perspective, which leads us to rejoice, once again, in our King. Thanksgiving is a recognition that you do not possess anything in yourself, that everything comes as a gift from a loving God. When you do that, you recognize, that God gave these things to us for our enjoyment and enrichment. He did not give them that we might practice denial of them; He wanted us to have them. But God wanted us to have them in ways that do not feed our ego and minister to our self-importance; and the only way that we can do so is to receive them with thanksgiving.

That is what "because it is consecrated by the word of God and prayer" means. Consecration means to put something to its proper use, and thus to render it safe for you to use. The habit of giving thanks accomplishes that.

When you take everything as a gift of God, your life, your breath, your family, your friends, your clothing, your food, your circumstances, your trials, your pressures, and your problems and thank God for them, then they are rendered safe. You no longer are the king on the throne, dictating to the rest of the world how to behave; you are a humble recipient of the gift from the Father's hand. Grateful people recognize God's provisions in their lives!!!

Father, thank You for this day and the breath we breathe and gift of life today. Lord, open the storehouses of heaven and pour out Your abundant blessings over us and our family today. Lord, thank You for *all* that You have given us to sustain our day. Lord, thank You for my friends and family. Lord, we are grateful for Your love, Your mercy, and the gift of eternal life.

Lord, use us to teach others to have a thankful heart and to share this gratitude we have with them.

Father, we love You. Amen.

NOTES

WAIT PATIENTLY

I remain confident of this: I will see the goodness of the LORD in the land of the living. Wait for the LORD; be strong and take heart and wait for the LORD.

Psalm 27:13–14, NIV

As Joshua prepared to take over the leadership of Israel and to replace Moses, God told him to be strong and courageous. He repeatedly told him to put his trust in God and not in himself, his armies, or the nations around him. Then he would win the victories over his enemies.

As we prepare for our daily battles with Satan and the things this life can throw at us, we are told to trust in God who will give us the strength to overcome. Paul said he could do all things through Jesus Christ who gave him strength, and we can live with this same confidence. We are told to live without anxiety or fear of tomorrow. As we learn to trust in God and live in His power, we will rid ourselves of many of the worries that plague us each day. Jesus said that each day has enough trouble of its own. So when we worry about things, we are just adding unnecessary stress to our lives that causes doubts and fear without doing anything positive for us.

As we face a new day, let each of us determine to give our cares to the Lord, and as we follow His will, we will have joy and peace. We will pray for wisdom to do what we can do, and then when we have done this, we will wait on the Lord for results. We will not fill our minds with what might happen or regrets of what might have been, but rather with that which is true, noble, right, pure, lovely, and admirable. And then the God of peace will be with us.

Not only does God call on us to wait, but to do so patiently. If we will take Him up on this practice, there will come a bravery that only comes from being clothed in His glorious presence. In and through each and every season of our lives, the Holy Spirit will give us courage to fulfill the good, pleasing, and perfect will of God our Father. We are facing a very dark and evil time in our world today. There is an evil that is ravaging the entire world, bringing disease and death and financial adversity and fear. Yet, we are reminded that "in times of disaster, [we] will not wither; in days of famine [we] will enjoy plenty" (Ps. 37:19, NIV).

In such a time as this, we are also reminded to worship and rise, to prevail. Be brave and courageous, and never lose hope. Yes, keep on waiting—for God will never disappoint us!!!

Father, thank You for this day and for waking us up and setting us on our journey. Lord, let Your abundant blessings flow mightily over us and our family today. Lord, as we are overwhelmed with the cares and worries of the world, help us look to You and turn them over to You. Lord, keep us from trying to carry the weight of the world on our own shoulders, because we know we are not able to bear it all. Lord, use us to bear the burdens of those around us when we have the opportunity to do so.

Father, we love You. Amen.

NOTES

HOMECOMING

And I heard a loud voice from heaven saying, "Behold, the tabernacle of God is with men, and He will dwell with them, and they shall be His people. God Himself will be with them and be their God. And God will wipe away every tear from their eyes; there shall be no more death, nor sorrow, nor crying. There shall be no more pain, for the former things have passed away." Then He who sat on the throne said, "Behold, I make all things new." And He said to me, "Write, for these words are true and faithful.

Revelation 21:3–5, NKJV

The first book of the Bible begins with an intimate interaction between God and man, and the last book ends in a similar fashion, with God Himself wiping every tear from our eyes. What a way to end the story! With our heavenly Father bringing us on His knee to wipe away every tear from our eyes. Maybe at that moment we will realize that we are finally home. I wonder if the tears we shed will be a mixture of joy at being in the Father's presence and relief that there will be no more death or mourning or crying or pain. Whatever the reason for our tears, the soothing comfort of a Father's love will assuredly take away all our pain and make all our suffering but a distant memory.

We have this promise, that at the end of all time, we will find ourselves in the arms of the Father. He will come and live with us and be our God, and we will live with Him and be His people. May this be the hope that we cling to for those who have gone before us in Christ and for us as well. While our temporal life on earth may soon come to an end, we have the hope of an eternity living near to the Father's heart.

Never forget that we have God's indwelling Spirit of comfort, who is with us the moment each solitary teardrop starts to dampen our lashes. Jesus came to heal the brokenhearted and set the captive free, and His Holy Spirit understands. He knows, He loves, and He cares for each one of us, so draw closer to His arms of comfort, and trust in His love today, for a day is coming where there will no longer be any mourning, crying, or pain.

We may not understand why we have to endure some of the things in life that cause such heartache and pain, but let us never forget that His eternal perspective is broader than our restricted view. He is our present help in trouble today, and tomorrow He will wipe away the tears from all of our eyes!!!

Father, thank You for this day and the strength to press in, press through, and press on in it. Lord, open the windows of heaven and shine down Your abundant blessings upon us and our family today. Lord, we thank You that soon there will be no more death or mourning or crying or pain. Lord, we know that You have promised to wipe away every tear from our eyes. Lord, we look forward to that day when we will see You face-to-face and be with You forever. Lord, use us to be the hand of Your love that someone needs today.

Father, we love You. Amen.

NOTES

ASK, SEEK, AND KNOCK

Ask, and it will be given to you; seek, and you will find; knock and it will be opened to you. For everyone who asks receives, and he who seeks finds, and to him who knocks it will be opened.

Matthew 7:7–8, NKJV

I love the promise of this passage. Ask and you will receive; seek and you will find; knock and the door will be opened for you. All who ask, seek, and knock will be satisfied. You know, though, sometimes asking and seeking and knocking does not receive an instant answer; sometimes, we have to persevere and hope and in faith keep asking, keep seeking, keep knocking.

In asking, seeking, and knocking, we can be assured and confident that God holds our life in His loving hands, that He has a plan and a purpose for our lives, and that He is good. He knows the times and seasons. The circumstances and reasons. Keep asking, seeking, and knocking and in all, keep trusting. It's not bad to keep asking and keep seeking and keep knocking, because in that process we draw closer to God, see things from His perspective, and align our hearts with His plans and purposes.

Sometimes I wonder if that is the point, that in the asking, seeking, and knocking we find God, not just the answers to our prayers, that it's all about the *Giver*, not the getting. We may be asking but are we seeking and knocking? God delights to give to the one who will receive. Ask, seek, and knock.

There is an intensity, a deep desire to see the door open; to claim all that is ours in Christ, the focus is on God's will, His kingdom, and His glory, on our most basic needs, daily bread, and on overcoming sin through forgiveness and deliverance. Jesus is reminding us that if we stay after these, not only will we get what we ask for, but we will also be changed in the process. God is a good, good Father!!!

Father, thank You for this day and the breath of Your Word and prayer. Lord, let Your abundant blessings pour out over us and our family today. Lord, thank You so much for the many prayers You have answered. Thank You, Lord, for answering our prayers to be more like You as we grow in an intimate relationship with You. Lord, we confess we are still so very far from Your perfection, but when we look at the distance You have brought us in the past, we can view the future only with excitement knowing that You will lead us on to become more like You in the future. Lord, use us to help others to seek, ask, and find You.

Father, we love You. Amen.

NOTES

CHILDLIKE

At that time the disciples came to Jesus, saying, "Who then is greatest in the kingdom of heaven?" Then Jesus called a little child to Him, set him in the midst of them, and said, "Assuredly, I say to you, unless you are converted and become as little children, you will by no means enter the kingdom of heaven. Therefore whoever humbles himself as this little child is the greatest in the kingdom of heaven.

Matthew 18:1–4, NKJV

As I read these scriptures, I really began to think about what it means to become like a child. What qualities do children possess that adults do not? The first one that came to my mind was trust.

While I realize there may have been many more whom our Savior was referring to, trust seemed really important to me. Little children trust the adults in their life completely. They have complete confidence that they will be fed, clothed, cared for if they get hurt, and that parent will be there whenever they are needed.

How much simpler would our lives be if we would give our heavenly Father this same trust? After all, can't we have complete confidence in Him? Can't we trust that He will supply our every need?

What does this mean for us? I've said it before, and I'll say it again: total dependence is a hard one for me. But if we want to enter the kingdom, we have to become children. One of those qualities is total dependence on our heavenly Father. Trust that we will be fed, clothed, cared for, and He will always be there when we need Him.

Most of us want to know our life counts beyond the here and now. Jesus' closest followers wanted to know more than that; they wanted to be the greatest in His kingdom. Jesus constantly turns our ideas of power and influence upside down. Jesus tells us we must take the posture of children to enter God's kingdom and that our humility will ultimately impact our influence!!! Take a few minutes to ask God to show you how to take the posture of a child as you seek to know and follow Him!!!

Father, thank You for this day and Your amazing grace and mercy. Lord, open the floodgates of heaven and rain down your abundant blessings upon us and our family today. Lord, help us to become as a child. Lord, help us to put all our trust in You. Gracious Lord, our pride gets in the way. Lord, we are as challenged today by the image of Your holding a child before us as Your disciples were back then. Lord, teach us the difference between childlike and childish, and teach us anew what is most important in our lives. Lord, use us to be a light of Your love to all we meet today.

Father, we love You. Amen.

NOTES

FREEDOM

Live as free people, but do not use your freedom as a cover-up for evil; live as God's slaves.

1 Peter 2:16, NLT

Freedom is a wonderful gift that should be cherished, encouraged, and protected by people everywhere. All over the world, there are regions and nations where liberty is denied and justice is callously set aside. For freedom to be truly experienced, equality and dignity have to be made available and shared with everyone. Freedom can only work if people can express their views, opinions, or ideas in a biblical way and with unconditional love.

We may not agree with what people think or say, but if the thought process is to forcefully silence dissent or stridently suppress the opposition, then we are no longer free; instead, we are held captive to our choices and enslaved by our own prejudices.

When the apostle Peter was writing to the newly formed Christian churches, he wanted them to personally experience the freedom that Christ had obtained for humanity through His crucifixion. They were set free from the eternal consequences of their sins, so they could now live as a free people (freed from fear and liberated from guilt) whose response to this great grace from God should have been to love and forgive one another.

However, as Peter rightly cautioned those believers, they were also not to abuse their deliverance from damnation as a means of covering up evil. God had pardoned them through Jesus, but this did not mean they were now free to do what they liked or to justify their sins. It meant that they should respond by serving God faithfully, doing what He wanted, and sharing this great privilege of being forgiven.

Let's cherish our freedom by sharing our Christian faith in the best ways that we can: accepting and forgiving one another as well as listening to and loving each other!!!

Father, thank You for this day and Your mercy and grace. Lord, pour out Your abundant blessings over us and our family today. Lord, You commanded us to love God and one another. To truly practice this, we will have to overcome loathing and despising those whom we strongly oppose. Lord, help us to embrace and be changed by Your commands. Lord, open our hearts to Your Word today. Lord, we thank You for this gift of incredible redemption that leads to freedom. Lord, use us to love others in word and action today.

Father, we love You. Amen.

NOTES

OUR WEAKNESS, CHRIST'S STRENGTH

And He said to me. "My grace is sufficient for you, for My strength is made perfect in weakness." Therefore most gladly I will rather boast in my infirmities, that the power of Christ may rest upon me. Therefore I take pleasure in infirmities, in reproaches, in needs, in persecutions, in distresses for Christ's sake. For when I am weak, then I am strong.

2 Corinthians 12:9–10, NKJV

We will experience the power of God in our lives when our hearts catch fire with the Holy Spirit. His power enables us to be His witness throughout the world, accomplishing a mission we cannot carry out in our own strength.

Men and women throughout the centuries have been able to accomplish more than they could have imagined because the power of the Holy Spirit was at work in their lives. In this generation, we need Spirit-filled believers with hearts on fire who are willing to step beyond the boundaries of their own abilities.

We need believers who dare to do great and mighty works in the name of Christ and in His power as He leads them in life. Instead of living by fear, we must live by faith in what God says in His Word. Instead of falling into despair, we must engage in hope in the promises of God. Instead of worrying in our circumstances, we must be bold and courageous in the power of God.

Perhaps we will resolve to be one of the weak ones who hold to the promise of God for His power perfected in weakness, declaring with Paul, "When I am weak, then I am strong!" and adding, "I can't, but He can!" Oh that you and I could display that kind of dependence! But it isn't so far-fetched. It just takes intentional effort each time our weaknesses or hardships come into view.

Effort to forsake dependence on ourselves and put our trust in God alone. Did you notice that the more Paul boasts in his weaknesses, the more Christ's power rests on him? And the same is true for us!!!

Father, thank You for this day and the strength and grace to walk in it. Lord, pour out Your abundant blessings over us and our family today. Lord, open our eyes to how our weaknesses give You the opportunity to show others Your power through our witness. Lord, remind us that others are watching how we respond to the troubles and trials of life, and that they are looking for strength to overcome their own problems. Lord, use our lives to encourage others. Lord, use us to bless others through our hardships, and help us to smile and continue being faithful in spite of our weaknesses.

Father, we love You. Amen.

NOTES ________________________________

____

____

OUR FEAR, GOD'S STRENGTH

His pleasure is not in the strength of the horse, nor his delight in the legs of the warrior; the LORD *delights in those who fear him, who put their hope in his unfailing love.*

Psalm 147:10–11, NIV

If you were in charge of hiring someone to lead an entire nation through a wilderness, what qualities would be valuable? If you were hiring someone to take on a conquering army with a minimal force, would you look for courage, ability, and experience? Would you look for a great orator to deliver a solemn message from God to a nation? All of those qualities certainly are valid; you wouldn't send an inept person to do any of those jobs.

But our criteria and God's criteria must be different. He chose Moses, Gideon, and Jeremiah, and each one had reasons why they couldn't do what God told them to do. Moses said he couldn't talk; Gideon said he was too weak; and Jeremiah said he was too young! It's interesting that God's patience seemed a little pushed in each of those cases. He told each one that He would empower them to do what He wanted. I don't know what you value in a person, but God doesn't delight "in the strength of a horse" or "the legs of the warrior." If the strength of a powerful horse couldn't impress God, then no man, no matter how strong, would ever impress God.

In contrast, verse eleven tells us, "The LORD taketh pleasure in them that fear him, in those that hope in his mercy" (KJV). If you have strength, that is all the strength you are going to have. If you fear God, you will have all the strength that God has! We can never impress God by something we do, whether that is never making a mistake, or being brave enough, smart enough, etc. God is not impressed by what man is impressed with. Moses had fear; God had strength. Gideon had fear; God had strength. Jeremiah had fear; God had more power than he could dream of!

To impress God with our abilities is futile since He is the one who gave them to us in the first place! God can help the weakest person because He knows the weakest person. God values our fear rather than our strength.

When we fear God, we have all that we need, and we need not fear anything else. Remember today that God will not be impressed by how spiritual, smart, or strong we are; God is impressed by people who are impressed by Him. But God loves those who fear Him and put their hope in His unfailing love.

There's just one response of the human heart to which God reaches out: it's the response of faith, of love, and of commitment to Him. Don't rely on your ability and your own strength; they will fail you sooner or later. But put your trust in the unfailing love and faithfulness and the mercy of God. Put your hope in Him, and He will not fail you!!!

Father, thank You for this day and the strength to walk in it. Lord, let your abundant blessings flow like a mighty river over us and our family today. Lord, increase both our fear of You and our trust in Your unfailing love. Lord, keep us from ever allowing our thinking or our understanding to take the place of Your revealed Word. Lord, give us wisdom to understand Your will ahead of our own and the concerns of others ahead of our own interests. Lord, use us to be the touch of Your love that someone needs today.

Father, we love You. Amen.

NOTES

NO GREATER NAME

Therefore God exalted him to the highest place and gave him the name that is above every name, that at the name of Jesus every knee should bow, in heaven and on earth and under the earth, and every tongue acknowledge that Jesus Christ is Lord, to the glory of God the Father.

Philippians 2:9–11, NIV

Sometimes less is more. Today's scripture may be few in words, but the words used hold more than all the words mankind has ever uttered or even thought of! There truly is no MORE: no greater name than the name of Jesus. There is no other name by which a sin-sick soul is healed. There is no other name by which we can be saved! The name of Jesus . . . there is no other name that evokes such authority yet imparts such unspeakable love and mercy!

The Name of Jesus . . . above all other names, above all principalities, and above all powers! The name of Jesus, that precious name, will forever be our banner . . . in battle, in victory, in sweet retreat, in triumph! Jesus, Jesus, Jesus. There *is* something about that name!

When doubt or fear overwhelms you, just begin to speak the name that is above every name . . . the name of Jesus! When we think of Jesus, our thoughts should be enormous, without boundary, inexhaustible, incomprehensible, unmatchable, and unfathomable.

May today's few words be the richest words you've ever read . . . the name of Jesus is more than enough! Jesus, Jesus, Jesus . . . there is something special about Your name. As our lips speak forth Your Name, our hearts are overjoyed at the awareness of Your presence. Oh, how we love the name of Jesus; it is as honey on our lips, sweet, pure, and nourishing to our soul. May our mouths ever show forth Thy praise and our hearts sing of Thy goodness today and every day!!!

Father, thank You for this day and Your amazing grace. Lord, let Your abundant blessings flow from the floodgates of heaven over us and our family today. Lord, Your name is wonderful! Your sacrifice for our sin was so loving and generous. Lord, we're so thankful that our Father raised you from the dead and that through You, we will be able to be with God and worship You all eternity! Lord, You are glorious. Lord, use us to be a bold witness of Your saving grace to all we meet today.

Father, we love You. Amen.

NOTES

THE GREAT "COMMISSION" . . . NOT THE GREAT "SUGGESTION"

Then Jesus came to them and said, "All authority in heaven and on earth has been given to me. Therefore go and make disciples of all nations, baptizing them in the name of the Father and of the Son and of the Holy Spirit, and teaching them to obey everything I have commanded you. And surely I am with you always, to the very end of the age.

Matthew 28:18–20, NIV

To make disciples is the great command here given to all believers. This is not only for pastors and missionaries but also for every believer. This passage is often used to encourage us to evangelize and make converts.

While evangelism is important, this commission is about much more than just making converts. New believers must also be brought up in the faith or made into disciples. Notice also that we are commanded to make disciples of all nations. That includes the nation we live in, the nations around us, and every nation in the whole world. There is only one God and one way to be saved; therefore, all must be told.

There are two main parts to making disciples in this commission. The first is baptism and the second is teaching.

Baptizing is the outward sign and confession of believing and, therefore, being saved and entering the church. It is the result of evangelism and of faithfully calling people to faith and repentance. The second part of making disciples is by teaching. This teaching is to be done in both word and example. The focus of the teaching should be the commands and teachings of Jesus. Notice here that it says "all." We need to teach "all" that Christ taught, not just our pet texts and doctrines.

Before you can make disciples, you need to be a disciple. Disciples believe that Jesus has full authority in their lives. They believe Jesus is working today in this world through the Holy Spirit. They believe that what Jesus taught is true; he is the Son of God and the Savior of the world. The great comfort we have and our great hope for success is that Jesus is always with us and will continue to be with us wherever we go until the end of time.

The implication for our mission is clear. Making disciples means getting involved with people. Jesus' disciples hung out with Jesus in order to be sent out by Him. If we need these marching orders, if we get out of the shadow of our church buildings and culture. He will go with us! Glory!!!

Father, thank You for this day and for the breath of Your Word. Lord, let Your abundant blessings be on our family's portion today. Almighty God, I know you sent Jesus so the world could be saved. We know that means more than just them hearing about Jesus. Lord, we know You want people to be true followers, to be disciples. So forgive us, Father, for the times we have procrastinated because we worried the job was too big, too hard, too expensive, and too personally demanding. Lord, help us to be more excited and generous with sharing the gospel with others. Lord, use us to be a voice crying in the wilderness of this world that Jesus is the way, the truth, and the life.

Father, we love You. Amen.

NOTES

GUARDING YOUR SPIRITUAL HEART

He who trusts in his own heart is a fool, but whoever walks wisely will be delivered.

Proverbs 28:26, NKJV

I think we all know and understand why it's important to protect our physical heart. After all, it controls the flow of blood in the body, and proper blood flow is essential for survival. But the question I want to pose to you today is this: Why is it important to guard our spiritual heart?

I believe the Bible gives us three answers to that question. 1) Out of it are the issues of life. Proverbs 4:23 says: "Keep thy heart with all diligence; for out of it are the issues of life" (KJV). So, what exactly does that mean? It means that our thoughts, actions, attitudes, and feelings are all dependent on the condition of our heart. Everything we are and everything we do reflects what's in our heart. 2) It is the source of our words. Luke 6:45 reminds us: "A good man out of the good treasure of his heart bringeth forth that which is good; and an evil man out of the evil treasure of his heart bringeth forth that which is evil: for of the abundance of the heart his mouth speaketh" (KJV). The things that find their way into our heart will eventually find their way out of our mouths. 3) It is deceitful and desperately wicked: who can know it? The heart wants what the heart wants whether it's a good thing or not. Our hearts will lie to us.

They will promise us great things, but in the end, all we will receive are disappointment and guilt. It goes on to say in Proverbs 28:26: "He that trusteth in his own heart is a fool." We must guard our hearts against outside evil influences and even from itself. Our hearts cannot be our guide through life. That's God's place. Knowing this, is it any wonder God cautions us to daily take up our armor, including the breastplate of righteousness.

The world is out to get us. Satan is out to destroy us. Even our own flesh is against us. Every day is a spiritual battle, and we must be armed and ready to defend ourselves and our faith. Guard your heart today, my friend!!!

Father, thank You for this day and for waking us up and setting us on our journey through it. Lord, open the windows of heaven and shine down Your abundant blessings upon us and our family today. Lord, help us to remain planted in our present circumstances. Let us not grow comfortable or discontent. Lord, rather than checking out or becoming unsettled, remind us there is a higher purpose for what we are experiencing. Lord, use us to point others toward You today.

Father, we love You. Amen.

NOTES ____________________

LIFE LIGHT

Your word is a lamp to my feet and a light to my path.
Psalm 119:105, NKJV

Have you ever been walking somewhere at night with a flashlight and then suddenly the battery dies, and the light goes out? For a moment panic sets in, but if you wait a moment or two, your eyes will adjust to the dark and you will be able to see enough to continue most of the time, depending on your circumstances. As your eyes adjust, you can actually see things you could not with the flashlight as it is bright but only in a small, focused area.

The same applies to this scripture in the Psalms. Apart from God, we are walking in the dark spiritually speaking and can only see a short distance in front of us. As we come to trust in Jesus and follow in His footsteps, our path becomes easier to see, and we learn from the Scriptures how we should live and treat others.

In time, our heart becomes more like His and we can see things never seen before as the Holy Spirit speaks to our heart and mind and can further direct us where to go and what to do when we arrive. God's Word is alive with everything we need so we can see in the spiritual darkness that surrounds us and directs us to safety. We also become like a lighthouse to those stranded in that darkness and offer hope like a beacon of light in the midst of a storm.

The Bible truly illuminates our path to the Father, but we first must be willing to put down our flashlight and allow Him to adjust our spiritual eyes to see in a new light that is better than the one we have known. The Word of God is the Christian life support, our sustaining power, our oxygen tank, our feeding tube, our guiding light, and our eternal hope of glory.

Without the light of God's Word, we will continue to stumble in the dark. We will never make it to our destination because we will not be able to see our way out of where we are. It is the light of God's Word that illuminates our path!!!

Father, thank You for this day and the gift of the Holy Spirit. Lord, open the storehouses of heaven and let Your abundant blessings flow over us and our family today. Lord, thank You for giving us Your truth in Scripture. Lord, to know that You love us enough to communicate in language so we can hear and read Your message is truly awe inspiring. Lord, make our hearts hunger for Your truth revealed in Your Word. Lord, use us to be the light of Your love to those lost in the darkness.

Father, we love You. Amen.

NOTES

SPIRITUAL WEAPONS

For though we walk in the flesh, we do not war according to the flesh. For the weapons of our warfare are not carnal, but mighty in God for pulling down strongholds, casting down arguments and every high thing that exalts itself against the knowledge of God, bringing every thought into captivity to the obedience of Christ.

2 Corinthians 10:3–5, NKJV

Our commitment to Christ is the key to unlocking the ability to pull down the spiritual strongholds of Satan in our lives. What are spiritual strongholds? Paul defines them clearly for us in today's verses. Strongholds are "arguments and every high thing that exalts itself against the knowledge of God"—fortresses of lies against the truth of God in our lives.

As followers of Christ, we engage in spiritual warfare with the mighty weapons God provides. This spiritual struggle ensued long before we arrived on the scene, but we are not helpless in the face of evil. We take back spiritual ground that our enemy, Satan, has stolen from us and those we love.

We are not created to hide behind the walls of the church, to merely defend ourselves from the schemes of the devil. We are created to offensively establish God's kingdom here on earth, to ward off the fiery darts of the evil one, to make war in heavenly places, and to gain ground for the cause of Christ.

Jesus told us that the "kingdom of heaven suffers violence, and the violent take it by force" (NKJV).

This spiritual violence of which Jesus speaks describes how Satan strikes at us. He is intent on our defeat and our destruction; he sets out to disrupt, damage, and ultimately, destroy our lives. He will infiltrate our emotions, relationships, health, and finances. John 10:10 makes it plain that he comes to "steal, and to kill, and to destroy" (NKJV).

No matter the spiritual violence that he attempts to wreak on us, as believers, we can set him in full retreat through the power that we have through Jesus Christ. When we submit our lives to God, when we engage the mighty weapons God has given, and when we resist the devil, he will flee before us. We have authority through the name of Jesus, the power of His Word, and His overcoming blood. Our Savior will crush him under our feet and lead us to victory!!!

Father, thank You for this day and Your Word that gives us the authority and power to take all thoughts captive. Lord, open the floodgates of heaven and rain down Your abundant blessings upon us and our family today. Lord, make us bold in the power of Your light. Lord, help us take back territory that the enemy has stolen from us and those we love. Lord, lead us to engage the enemy with courage to advance Your kingdom here on earth. Lord, use us to be the breath of Your love to those in need of it.

Father, we love You. Amen.

NOTES

A CALL TO WAIT

He will swallow up death forever, And the Lord GOD will wipe away tears from all faces; the rebuke of His people, He will take away from all the earth; For the LORD has spoken. And it will be said in that day: "Behold, this is our God; We have waited for Him, and He will save us. This is the LORD; we have waited for Him; we will be glad and rejoice in His salvation."

Isaiah 25:8–9, NKJV

So much of life seems to be spent waiting. As a kid, you're constantly waiting to be a certain age to be able to participate in certain things. You wait in lines, you wait on people, you wait for a special day to arrive. You wait and wait and wait and wait and wait . . . will the waiting ever end? And more importantly, will it have been worth it?

Much of the relationship with the Lord is described as a call to wait. We are to wait for the Lord, which is another way of saying we trust Him. Waiting does not mean we are idle in our relationship with God, but that we are actively trusting Him. The need to wait on the Lord arises from the fact that our experience does not currently align with His promises.

We are redeemed people waiting for the completion of redemption. This has been promised to us, and God will bring it about . . . but right now we wait . . . we trust . . . we hope. That day will come . . . the day when we no longer have to talk about waiting but will be able to speak in past tense and declare that we have waited.

The day of final salvation will come when all our waiting will seem like it has been no more than a few moments. Salvation will be complete, and all the waiting will be over. Yet, until then . . . we wait. Not idly, but expectantly. We wait in such a way that declares to the world our great confidence and trust in the Lord who is not idle but actively working toward the day for which we are waiting.

As we face difficult situations . . . difficult people . . . and difficulties in general, we know that He is always there with us, a strong tower to run to in time of need. A strong pair of arms to hold us and comfort us, and gentle, loving hands that extravagantly place before me a feat of rich food and wine—His Word, His Spirit—to nourish and bless us!!!

Father, thank You for this day and Your amazing grace to walk in it. Lord, pour out Your abundant blessings like a mighty river over us and our family today. Lord, thank You for always being there when we need You . . . and even when we think we don't. Lord, we're so glad You've got our backs. Lord, You know what lies ahead for us, what difficulties we will face each coming day, and You've already prepared all that we will need to get through each situation. Lord, we long for the day when death will be swallowed up forever, for the day when "disgrace" is not a word in our vocabulary. Lord, because you have restored honor and dignity, help us to grab hold of all You've laid out on

Your beautiful banquet table for me today. Lord, use us to be the light of Your presence to those who come our way.

Father, we love You. Amen.

NOTES

GOD'S HANDIWORK

The heavens declare the glory of God; the skies proclaim the work of his hands. Day after day they pour forth speech; night after night they reveal knowledge.

Psalm 19:1–2, NIV

We don't always need words to get our message across. The skies "pour forth speech" and "reveal knowledge" but have no words; nevertheless, "their voice goes out into all the earth." God's handiwork is revealed to all.

From the busiest, crowded city to the remotest, inaccessible places of the world, God has made it possible for everyone to know Him. Likewise, our lives speak to those around us, whether we use words or not. The way we spend our time, the way we spend our money, and tell people what we value pours forth a message.

God's presence in our lives also speaks to those around us. The fruit of His Spirit within us will touch others with its sweetness. His refining work in our lives speaks volumes. Many ignore the declaration of the glory of God in His handiwork, and they will ignore it in our lives too.

However, it's not our job to convict others of their need for God, but rather for our lives to show how good it is to live under God's government—to create curiosity, desire, and a longing for something more. Yet, if we're not convinced God's way is best, that His love is sufficient and His purposes good, then we won't attract anyone else to this way of life.

Our words will never be enough; there has to be a lifestyle that matches our beliefs. God speaks continually in His creation, sending forth a message to us about Himself. You learn about His craftsmanship and limitless all-powerful ability just by looking at what He has made. As you gaze on all He has created, you hear and see the wondrous declarations of His glory!!!

Father, thank You for this day and setting us on our journey through Your created path. Lord, open the windows of heaven and shine down Your abundant blessings upon us and our family today. Lord, Creator of the countless heavens and our own small blue planet, thank You for noticing the heart cries of us who are so small in a universe so large. Lord, we love You, admire You, trust You, and worship You with wonder. Lord, be exalted in our lives, our words, and our deeds this day. Lord, use us to be a bold witness of Your saving grace to all we meet today.

Father, we love You. Amen.

NOTES ______________________________

____

____

____

____

IN STEP

In their hearts humans plan their course,
but the Lord establishes their steps.

Proverbs 16:9, NIV

From the moment we come crying into this world, we begin to perform our duty. We assume our role in the plan of God and in the ordination of God. We begin the journey of life.

Whatever our background and whatever the journey ahead of us, none can escape the orchestration and arrangement that God has in store, and none are in control of their destiny, for only He who rules over all things is capable of such work.

Since the day man came into existence, God has been steady in His work, managing this universe and directing the change and movement of all things. Like all things, man quietly and unknowingly receives the nourishment of the sweetness and rain and dew from God. Like all things, man knowingly lives under the orchestration of God's hand.

The heart and spirit of man are held in the hand of God. If you believe this, any and all things, living or dead, will shift, change, renew, and disappear according to God's thoughts. This is how God rules over all things.

This proverb also speaks to how there will be moments in our lives when we face trials and hard times. Even in those circumstances, God is still very much present and all that is happening has been planned out by Him.

This proverb provides for us an all-encompassing picture of who God is in terms of how we ought to live and the control He has over this world. Let us daily pursue living for Him and place Him at the center of hearts, so when we take steps in life, He is the one who will be directly leading and guiding us to live for Him and His Glory!!!

Father, thank You for this day and the breath of life to experience it. Lord, let Your abundant blessings be our family's portion today. Lord, we know only You possess the power to direct our steps. Lord, we pray that our plans would align with Your plans for our lives. Lord, we know and trust that the plans You have for us are good. Lord, we pray that You will direct each and every one of our steps, allowing us to be influenced by the Spirit and Your grace. Lord, may all our steps glorify You, and may we never doubt the plans You have for us. Lord, let us be the touch of Your mercy and grace that someone needs today.

Father, we love You. Amen.

NOTES

REDEEMED

In him we have redemption through his blood, the forgiveness of sins, in accordance with the riches of God's grace that he lavished on us. With all wisdom and understanding, he made known to us the mystery of his will according to his good pleasure, which he purposed in Christ, to be put into effect when the times reach their fulfillment—to bring unity to all things in heaven and on earth under Christ.

Ephesians 1:7–10, NIV

There is a beautiful idea here in this section of Scripture—and that idea is redemption! It is as if someone who was a slave was transferred to a new master, but the old master pays a handsome price to have that slave redeemed and brought back into his own family!

That is the theme that is packed up here in these few verses from Ephesians 1. How does God redeem us? How does God buy us for Himself? How does God purchase us to be His own? We have been redeemed at the cost of God's own Son! And although the blessings of redemption are things that we presently enjoy, they include so much more than that!

We have yet to see redemption in its fullest glory! The Lord is working in us to conform us more and more to His image, and to bring us out of slavery. And one day, all things will be made new! Jesus Christ, through His own blood, will ultimately redeem all things to Himself, and bring them back together again—perfectly.

Praise God that our redemption is not just something we enjoy in the here and now! Paul says in Ephesians 1 that the redemption that Christians experience in Christ is actually one of the greatest spiritual blessings we can receive. To be Christ's possession is to have our sins forgiven, meaning we won't face the same judgment that awaits those who are not in Christ.

To be redeemed includes giving us assurance of the grace of God—that we can be certain of our salvation not because of how good we behave, but simply because of what God has done for us in Christ. In all these ways, Christ demonstrates His love for us.

As a result of that, our main response should be gratitude. Gratitude, then, lays the groundwork for holiness and devotion. Pray that the Lord would bury the hope and the joy of redemption in our hearts; and pray that we would see this redemption worked out in our families, lives, communities, nation, and the world!!!

Father, thank You for this day and for the strength and confidence to walk through it. Lord, let Your abundant blessings pour out over us and our family today. Lord, for those of us who believe, I pray that, this morning, our hearts would be newly awakened to the wonder of the cross. Lord, for those of us who have received such grace, I pray that the eyes of our heart would be enlightened to the glory of His grace. And I pray that from this we would experience the freedom He has fully purchased, and that in this freedom we would live to the praise of His glorious grace. Lord, use us to be a voice crying out prepare the way of the Lord. He is coming back to this lost and decaying world.

Father, we love You. Amen.

NOTES

LEARNER, FOLLOWER, AND DISCIPLER

The Lord G*OD has given me the tongue of a teacher, that I may know how to sustain the weary with a word. Morning by morning he wakens—wakens my ear to listen as those who are taught.*

Isaiah 50:4, NRSV

We live in a world where communication has advanced, but the human quality of this communication is deteriorating. It is against that backdrop that we, as disciples of the Lord, must spread His love around us.

To successfully carry out this mission, I invite you to meditate on Isaiah 50:4, which presents the secret of the Lord's servant: "The Lord God has given me the tongue of a teacher, that I may know how to sustain the weary with a word. Morning by morning he wakens—wakens my ear to listen as those who are taught." Thus, the servant of the Lord who communicates is known for using language for consolation, encouragement, recovery, and the communication of grace as affirmed by the apostle Paul in Ephesians 4:29: "Let no evil talk come out of your mouths, but only what is useful for building up, as there is need, so that your words may give grace to those who hear" (NRSV).

The tongue of a discipler is a gift from God, a gift that grows through developing intimacy with Him and communicating His wonders. Intimacy with the Master is the secret of the servant of the Lord. It's achieved through morning listening, a fundamental characteristic of the Lord's disciple, who never begins a day without spending time at the feet of the Lord. Each morning, the disciple wants to hear the voice of the Lord, who indicates which road to follow. This listening will develop the follower into a good disciple who is always ready to learn from the Master.

It is a time for the servant of the Lord as He communicates that His wonders can be compared to a river where water is flowing, rather than a backwater where it is stored. This means that what the disciple has received from the Lord is shared with others and that the disciple will receive more. The disciple is characterized by the desire for and the practice of communicating joy, peace, tranquility, love, comfort, and communicating life around us. Indeed, the Lord is always ready to teach His disciple who finds time to meet Him.

To be a blessing to those who are weary, you must first "open your ears" to God's gentle voice. He will both encourage and instruct you. He will reveal His love, unveil His truth, and give knowledge for yourself and others. But it is imperative that we listen!!!

Father, thank You for this day and the breath of life found in Your Word. Lord, help us to listen this morning, and every morning give us to You, as You guide our path. Lord, we do not want the form of religion, but the heart, life, and attitude of You. Lord, we need Your deep motivation to stir our lives.

Lord, please eradicate our warped images and renew our understanding of Your zeal to obey, care for the lost, desire to fellowship with God, and be earnest in hearing from God. Lord, use us to be a learner, follower, and reproducer of You to those who need to be discipled.

Father, we love You. Amen.

NOTES

PRESS IN, PRESS THROUGH, AND PRESS ON

My brethren, count it all joy when you fall into various trials, knowing that the testing of your faith produces patience. But let patience have its perfect work, that you may be perfect and complete, lacking nothing.

James 1:2–4, NKJV

The definition of "perseverance" is "Steadfastness, constancy, endurance; or a patient waiting." According to this passage, trials test our faith. And faith develops perseverance, which is necessary if we are going to be spiritually mature. Most believers would likely agree with this truth.

But what about the joy? How many of us consider it pure joy to develop perseverance? The problem for many of us isn't a lack of knowledge. The problem is a divided heart. In order to find joy in the midst of trials, Christ and His glory must be the objects of our heart's affection. In every situation, our goal must be to know Him more and to reflect His character. Only when this is true can we have joy when our faith is being tested.

Perseverance is not easy. Just ask any long-distance runner. It hurts to keep running when everything in you longs to stop. The motivation to continue is the reward. The same is true spiritually. Considering the joy to face trials does not mean that we enjoy the hardship. God is not asking us to be happy to have cancer or to lose a job. Jesus was not happy when He went to the cross . . . but "for the joy set before Him" He endured. The joy comes because our hearts are fixed on Jesus—He is our reward. And to be mature in Him we must learn to persevere.

So if you are struggling to have joy when your faith is tested, examine your heart. Where do your affections lie? Take heart and persevere! The reward is worth the hardship. Sometimes reading a passage from the Bible in a translation other than the one you are used to can really give you fresh insight.

Here, what caught me off guard was how the New Revised Standard Version (NRSV) phrased a familiar verse speaking of how to deal with trials in this life, saying that we should "consider it nothing but joy." I am used to reading "count it all joy." But "consider it nothing but joy" is a new understanding for me. Instead of knowing that the trial was a bad thing that I was supposed to dress up as a good thing (counting it as joy), I am actually supposed to not even think anything about the trial was bad, but rather see through the apparent badness to the joy that it was meant to bring. Nevertheless, let's try to see our trials as God's precious gift to us, His way of helping us grow to be like Him. And for that, we can rejoice!!!

Father, thank You for this day and Your amazing mercy and grace. Lord, let Your abundant blessings fall like rain from the floodgates of heaven upon us and our family today. Unchangeable and unshakeable God, through the friends You have sent into our lives and by the power of Your gift, the Holy Spirit, help us to stand up under trial and prove our character true with perseverance when under fire. Lord, give our faith courage and endurance so our lives show forth Your enduring strength. Lord, use us to be the strength of Your love that someone needs today.

Father, we love You. Amen.

NOTES

LIVE ONE DAY AT A TIME

So teach us to number our days, that
we may gain a heart of wisdom.

Psalm 90:12, NKJV

Too often we think in terms of years and make plans for the far distant future, and yet we are instructed to live one day at a time and not to even worry ourselves about the needs of tomorrow, for each day has sufficient trouble of its own.

We should not only reflect on the brevity of our time here on earth and recognize that our times are in God's hands and that He has scheduled every day of our life to bring glory to Himself, but also that we should make the best use of our time, during our brief sojourn on earth, by redeeming the time and making the most of every opportunity we have on earth.

This world is not our home for we have a heavenly citizenship and a glorious inheritance secured for us in heaven. But every day of our lives is an opportunity that God has graciously given us to use wisely and diligently for His glory, for the victorious life that has been lived wisely, and well is the one who has honored the Lord in thought, word, and deed.

May God teach each one of us to number our days carefully, so we may develop wisdom in our hearts by faith in Christ Jesus, our Savior. May we all count our days, and then consider with godly wisdom how we invest our time here. One day this will all be gone, and only that which is of eternal value will last. I pray that our lives will be invested in the eternal, and not in that which perishes like the grass. We are not given another year simply to take up space.

Wherever we may find ourselves as we end this year and start a new one, God wants to use each one of us. Let us never forget how Nehemiah teaches us that it is never too late for a new beginning!!!

Father, thank You for this day and each day of our lives and for the opportunities that You have given us to live a life, as unto You. Lord, let Your abundant blessings be our family's portion today. Lord, may each day of our lives, from this day forward, be exercised in a way that is pleasing to You, so that in all we say and do You may be glorified. Lord, teach us to make the most of the time we have; teach us to effectively utilize the life we have been given. Lord, may we accomplish all of the purposes that You have set out for us. Lord, teach us to number each and every one of our days. Lord, use us to be a bold witness of Your glory to all today.

Father, we love You. Amen.

NOTES

A NEW HEART

I will give you a new heart and put a new spirit within you; I will take the heart of stone out of your flesh and give you a heart of flesh. I will put My Spirit within you and cause you to walk in My statutes, and you will keep My judgments and do them.

Ezekiel 36:26–27, NKJV

The heart with its intentions is the eternal core of our being and the precious part of us that distinguishes us as creatures made in God's image; only God and human beings have a spirit. It is only with our heart that we can genuinely love and worship, and this is why our praise and service mean nothing to God if they don't come from the heart.

An important clarification is that the heart, as the Bible speaks of it, is not our feelings, but our power to choose a course of action. Spirit is "unbodily" personal power, the power we have in life to choose, take initiative, and express creativity.

God has created us to take dominion with Him and for Him in His kingdom, to be creative under Him. It is in the heart (spirit or will) that real change must begin. God sends His Word and Spirit to us, and we respond by putting our faith, trust, and confidence in Him, leaning the whole weight of our being in Christ.

As we connect with Christ, we come alive with His abundant, eternal, God kind of life. Our hearts can be good or bad.

The proud heart is hard and unreceptive to God as the good soil is to seed, listening, trusting, and responding to His initiative by sprouting with loving obedience. The spirit that trusts God and is brought to life through faith in Christ by God's Spirit, is well directed in spiritual fervor, rejoicing to overflow with love for God and others, including strangers and enemies.

When Christ lives in us, we cannot do what we used to do, nor do we want to. We cannot use the language we once did, nor can we think about sin in the same way. With our new heart, all we are changed, we become a people after God's own heart!!!

Father, thank You for this day and that You are good and gracious, long-suffering, and tenderhearted toward all Your children. Lord, open the storehouses of Your abundant blessings and rain them down upon us and our family today. Lord, Your never-failing promises to Your people are such a reassurance. Lord, thank You that we are part of Your body and that You have told us the end from the beginning, and thank You that all Your promises are yes and amen. Lord, teach us Your ways and keep us from straying from the path of holiness. Lord, thank You for Your indwelling Holy Spirit of life, who guides us into all truth. Lord, use us to be someone's blessing today.

Father, we love You. Amen.

NOTES

IMMANUEL

Therefore the Lord Himself will give you a sign: Behold, the virgin shall conceive and bear a Son, and shall call His name Immanuel.

Isaiah 7:14, NKJV

In light of a busy world, Jesus invades humanity with a God-sized announcement. We could focus on so many things of this verse of the coming Savior. We could look at the power of the immaculate conception.

We could hone in on the God who wanted to be found by giving seekers a sign. In this chaotic world Jesus as given a new name. He was given the name Immanuel, which means God is with us. Since sin entered the world, we have been in desperate need of a Messiah. There was nothing we were able to do by ourselves to be saved.

The blood of the animal sacrifices performed in the Old Testament only covered the sin. We needed the perfect Lamb, the Savior and the Messiah, to shed His blood to take our sins away completely. There is so much love in this verse. Isaiah knew what it was like to warn and instruct God's people, but the Lord also wanted His people to receive His comfort.

God's command for Isaiah was to comfort His people. He spoke tender, loving words to announce that their inequities were pardoned, that they didn't have to fight anymore to be clean. The people were about to face the Assyrians taking them to captivity, and they needed all the comfort God could provide.

The virgin would conceive and bear a child. The Savior would be born. The sin would be forgiven. My eyes fill with tears when I look back to my life without Jesus. I can't believe God decided to love me. I can't believe Jesus died for someone like me, that He bore my many sins. I didn't deserve it. And yet, the Messiah was born to give me and you life.

My friend, this was the greatest over answer of any prayer in history! The people had cried, "Send us a deliverer," hoping for some man, but God answered, "I'll give you a man. And yes, He would be a deliverer—for all mankind!" God over-answered by promising Immanuel! It's one thing to know God is with us; it's another to carry this truth into each day. Today, let the knowledge that God is with us lead us to love more fully, give more generously, and live more confidently!!!

Father, thank You for this day and Your amazing mercy and grace. Lord, pour out Your abundant blessing over us and our family today from Your storehouse. God, thank You that You loved us so much that You sent Your only Son to pay the price of our sin; Our hearts are full of praise of gratitude. Lord, thank You for the truths that are contained in Your Holy Word. Jesus, thank You that You walked the earth as a man, and you understand the limitations of our humanity. Lord, use us to share the true meaning of the birth of a risen Savior to all we meet today.

Father, we love You. Amen.

NOTES

PROMISED SEED

And behold, you will conceive in your womb and bring forth a Son, and shall call His name JESUS*. He will be great, and will be called the Son of the Highest; and the Lord God will give Him the throne of His father David.*

Luke 1:31–32, NKJV

It was the seed of the woman that was to crush the serpent's head. The promised seed had passed through the generations, first through Seth to Noah, then from Abraham to the sons of Jacob, via Ruth to David, and on and on through the royal line until Christ was born of Mary. She was to name Him Jesus, for He was both the stem and the root of Israel's greatest king, David. He was David's greater Son, the Lion of the tribe of Judah, the Lord Jesus Christ, Son of God, and son of Mary.

Although the reach of redemption was to encompass the whole earth (for the grace of God is without measure and beyond our understanding) it was the little nation of Israel through whom the seed was to be secretly transported so He could fulfill God's promises and prophecies to unite the divided kingdom of Judah and Israel, into one glorious kingdom, and to save that little nation from their sins. His office may be that of "Christ" for He is the anointed of God, and His title may be "Lord" for He is high and lifted up and His train fills the temple, but His name shall be called Jesus for He shall save His people Israel from their sins. And so, through Him all the families of the earth shall be blessed, for whosoever trusts in Him as Savior, Jew or Gentile, male or female, old or young, black or white, slave or free—all have the right to become the children of God who believe on His name.

The seed of greatness is inside believers in Christ because we have the DNA of Jesus within us. Remember that through Christ in us, the hope of glory, we are born again. We have the Holy Spirit inside us, the spirit of greatness. We are designed to be great. The environment we live in or the circumstances that surround us have nothing to do with the potential that is inside us. We are designed to impact the world.

After we are long gone, the world is meant to remember that we believers of Christ Jesus once lived here. Our expected end is greatness; that is the thought that God has for us. So what is stopping us to go for it? Let's proclaim the good news. His name is Jesus!!!

Father, thank You for this day and the reason for the season, Your Son is Jesus. Lord, open the floodgates of heaven and rain down Your abundant blessings over us and our family today. Lord, thank You for these eternal truths. They are overwhelming to us, and we praise You that You have revealed them to us in Your Word. Lord, they will be meaningless unless we live consistently with them. So, Lord, may we be a people known for their adoration and their service and their love for the King. Lord, thank You for coming into our world to save us and give us hope. Even in our pain, fill us with joy and amazement. Lord, use us to be the power of Your love to all today.

Father, we love You. Amen.

NOTES

MIRACULOUS CONCEPTION

And the angel answered and said to her, "The Holy Spirit will come upon you, and the power of the Highest will overshadow you; therefore, also, that Holy One who is to be born will be called the Son of God."

Luke 1:35, NKJV

Jesus is the Son of God and holy because he was conceived in the womb of Mary through the power of the Most High, revealed to us as the Holy Spirit. This conception is not something we can understand logically.

It is something we recognize as a miracle of God's power and reflective of God's divine love. Even believing in this miraculous conception is impossible, and only as both a gift and a miracle of God's grace does it come from the conviction of the Holy Spirit upon our hearts.

If we believe that Jesus is God come in human flesh, we know that the truth of this story had to begin in a miracle that is both incomprehensible and yet very simple. God took on human flesh as a baby named Jesus. This baby was conceived and carried in the womb of an ordinary young woman.

This miracle of conception reveals the character and compassion of the Most High God to bridge the distance from His heavenly perfection to our human mortality. While we may not fully understand it, we can receive its truth by grace.

Let's ask the Holy Spirit who brought this miracle to Mary to open all hearts of those who doubt this miracle and help them join with all who share the wonder of God's love, mercy, and grace. For in His humanity Jesus was to be the child born of Mary. I

n His deity Christ was to be the Son of the Highest. For unto us the child who was formed in the womb of Mary was to be born into the human race, but also unto us the Son of the most high God is given. GLORY! Awe is appropriate!

This story of Jesus encourages our hearts. It's as if Gabriel has come to each of us saying, "Rejoice! God is making you great." We too can choose to accept our role as servant and trust the Holy Spirit's power to overshadow ours. Please join me in surrendering to God by praying that His will be done according to His Word. Let's ask God that we may have the spirit of a servant too!!!

Father, thank You for this day and blessing of the Holy Spirit in our lives. Lord, open the windows of heaven and shine down Your abundant blessings upon us and our family today. Lord, thank You that You take the simple things of life and servants who are humble in spirit to be lifted up and used to Your praise and glory. Lord, we pray that we would walk humbly before You all the days of our lives and that You would use us in whatever way You choose. Lord, use us to share the good news of Christ Jesus today.

Father, we love You. Amen.

NOTES

THREE GIFTS

But while he thought about these things, behold, an angel of the Lord appeared to him in a dream, saying, "Joseph, son of David, do not be afraid to take to you Mary your wife, for that which is conceived in her is of the Holy Spirit. And she will bring forth a Son, and you shall call His name Jesus, *for He will save His people from their sins."*

Matthew 1:20–21, NKJV

Are we wondering how God is going to show up and reveal His saving power over these troubled difficult times in our lives? In verse twenty, notice the word "behold." Matthew uses this word as an indicator that something big is about to happen.

It's Matthew's way of saying, "Check this out! You're not going to believe what happens next!" The event, which at first seemed so tragic to Joseph, was the Creator coming into the world to save the world from its sins! God was working through Joseph's crisis for His purposes.

No matter how difficult our circumstances are today, let's seek the Lord and trust in His saving power. And when God shows up in an amazing way, may we begin our testimony of His working in our lives with, "Check this out! You're not going to believe how God showed up! It was amazing because He is amazing!"

Most Christians know the three gifts of the wise men to Jesus were gold, frankincense, and myrrh. But did you know that the angel of the Lord also gave Joseph the assurance that God is giving three gifts in sending Jesus? God's three gifts in Jesus are: 1) a Son of David who fulfills God's promise of a King who will reign forever; 2) a child who is God's Son, conceived by the Holy Spirit; and 3) a Great Deliverer, who will save his people from their sins.

There is no gift more precious or far-reaching than the gift of Jesus, God's Son and our Savior. The hope of the world was born into the family of Joseph, who was a humble carpenter. Through the child whom Joseph cared for, our salvation was accomplished. It was accomplished through the death of Jesus, who redeemed us from our sins and transferred us from the kingdom of darkness into the kingdom of His glorious light.

It guides us in the darkness and is a defense in danger. It sustains the fainting heart and overcomes the power of death. It bestows eternal life and exalts us to sit in heavenly places. It lifts us up out of the miry clay and sets our feet forever on Jesus, who is the Rock of our Salvation!!!

Father, thank You for this day and Your gift of salvation through Jesus. Lord, pour out Your abundant blessings over us and our family today. Lord, thank You for Your assurance and love, for people of faith who believe and act on Your Word, and for the Holy Spirit who leads us in Your will. Lord, help us to be so oriented that we allow our lives to be turned inside for the greater good of others. Lord, make us a servant in our hearts so that we do not count the cost but rather find it a privilege and honor to serve others. Lord, use us to be a voice of the gospel of Your grace to all who come our way today.

Father, we love You. Amen.

NOTES

GOD IS FAITHFUL

Sovereign Lord, as you have promised, you may now dismiss your servant in peace. For my eyes have seen your salvation, which you have prepared in the sight of all nations: a light for revelation to the Gentiles, and the glory of your people Israel.

Luke 2:29–32, NIV

"You can't teach an old dog new tricks" is a saying that many accept as an excuse for becoming staid and cynical as they age. I don't know about you, but I'm no dog. I believe I can change or better yet, I believe that God's Spirit can transform me. Here was the aged Simeon, old eyes and all, yet he was the one who got to see God's new light dawn for Israel. Why? Because Simeon believed God would do something great in his day. He kept believing in God's promises even when he was old. God still longs to do glorious things in our day.

This desire is true whether we are old, young, or in between! So let's keep believing, listening, trusting, following, and expecting Jesus to act in mighty ways. God is faithful. He longs to surprise us with glorious things in response to our prayers and our faith. As I read this story in Luke's Gospel, many things strike me. One of them is pretty obvious but seems worthy of our attention. I'm thinking of the way God works through people of all ages. Most strikingly, God was at work in Jesus, who was an infant in His first weeks of life. God was also at work in the parents of Jesus.

We don't know their precise ages, but it's likely that Mary was a teenage mother. Joseph was probably a bit older, but not in his nineties as some Christians once believed. If we take Jesus, Mary, and Joseph together, we will rightly conclude that God uses younger people in His work. But then there's Simeon. He was nearing the end of a life of faithfulness to God. He was eager for God's saving work through the promised Messiah. He was attentive to the leading of the Holy Spirit. He was bold both in prayer and in prophesying.

It's clear from the story that God used Simeon in a unique way, both to exalt Jesus and to warn the parents of Jesus that the future would not be easy. The story of Simeon reminds us that God is still using people of all ages. Sometimes we can assume that people close to the edges of life, both young and old, are not able to contribute in meaningful ways to this world, not to mention God's work in this world.

But God is not limited, and neither should we be limited by cultural biases. We are never too young, and we are never too old for God to use us in wonderful ways and to have great plans for our lives. If you're on the young side of life, or if you're on the old side, be open today to how God might use you in unexpected ways. If you're in the middle of life, pay attention to how those younger or older than you are making a difference!!!

Father, thank You for this day and the wonderful witness of this life of Simeon, who demonstrated a childlike trust in You and expected Your Word to be fulfilled to the letter. Lord, pour out Your abundant blessings over us and our family today. Lord, thank You that You are a light to us, and thank You that the light of Your love and forgiveness has shone into our hearts so that we are saved by grace through faith in You. Lord, no matter our age, may we be available to You. Use us in the work of Your kingdom, and help us not to discount the potential for any person of any age to make a difference.

Father, we love You. Amen.

NOTES

EVERLASTING LIFE

This is the will of the Father who sent Me, that of all He has given Me I should lose nothing, but should raise it up at the last day. And this is the will of Him who sent Me, that everyone who sees the Son and believes in Him may have everlasting life; and I will raise him up at the last day.

John 6:39–40, NKJV

Jesus simply and plainly states that everyone who looks to Him and believes in Him shall have eternal life. Is it really that simple? Can it be that simple? Of course. Our salvation is a free gift from God. It is not something we can earn. Our sins demand justice, demand punishment. The price we have to pay is eternity in hell. But Jesus paid the price for us; the godly died for the ungodly. And we simply must accept His gift, His free offer of salvation.

We cannot earn salvation, and we cannot do enough good to merit salvation; we simply accept it. However, once we accept that wonderful gift, our lives must change. When we realize the goodness, the graciousness of God, our focus becomes how to honor Him instead of ourselves. And we will want to live as one who shows our gratitude to God, who appreciates His gift, who points others to Him as well, to let them know about this great gift.

So often, people picture God as a surly old man looking for people who mess up so He can punish them. God's will, however, is that all come to salvation. He doesn't want any person to perish. He wants all to know Jesus and find salvation in Him. Jesus is the only way to God. Jesus is the door to a new and lasting life, not a temporary one, whether real or imagined. Jesus is the focus, the hope, and the life behind God's plan.

Learning to believe in Jesus is everything. Learning to see Jesus as God's Son is the doorway to forever. We receive a life that outlasts history and the assurance that nothing can ever conquer us once we belong to Jesus. He will raise us up in victory!!!

Father, thank You for this day and that Jesus is the Alpha and the Omega, the beginning and the end, and that we have been given forever in Him. Lord, open the floodgates of heaven and rain down Your abundant blessings upon us and our family today. Lord, fan our fires of faith and keep them vibrant in us. Lord, help us focus our eyes on You and trust You to lead us home. Lord, give us the wisdom to see through the doubts that Satan places before us. Lord, help us experience the eternal life that begins now and will never end. Lord, use us to share grace and mercy to those in need of it today.

Father, we love You. Amen.

NOTES ________________________________

____

____

SOLD OUT

While they were stoning him, Stephen prayed, "Lord Jesus, receive my spirit." Then he fell on his knees and cried out, "Lord, do not hold this sin against them." When he had said this, he fell asleep.

Acts 7:59–60, NIV

In the middle of his death, Stephen exemplified the character and fortitude of one sold out and abandoned to Christ. The only explanation for such a display of God's love during this unbelievable time is that Stephen had learned how to allow his spirit man to rule and reign in his life.

The story of Stephen is one of many found within the pages of the Bible that challenge us to look deep within and ask ourselves questions we have avoided in the past. The Holy Spirit presses us into face-to-face encounters with the truth of our spiritual walk.

What would we do if faced with the same situation as Stephen? Would we compromise our stance in Christ, or would we courageously stand our ground and receive the resulting consequences with grace and forgiveness? Could we stand up under the intense persecution, or would we buckle underneath the pressure?

Take a few minutes and reflect on this powerful story of Stephen. He was the first Christian martyred for his faith and as a result, the seeds of love and forgiveness planted at his death took root and brought a harvest in Saul of Tarsus. God took a man who witnessed and approved of Stephen's stoning and transformed him into one of the most influential men on earth, the apostle Paul.

We may never fully understand the impact our words and reactions have on those around us. Even in the most trying of times, there are people observing our behavior. Will they see the light of Christ shining from our faces? During your prayer time today, allow the Holy Spirit to delve into those deep places of your heart that remain locked down in soulish comfort zones. Give Him permission to bring you into a new level of radical abandonment.

We all need to come to the place where we are willing to lay it all on the line for Him. You have the power to forgive just as you have been forgiven. Each of us has sinned many more times against God than others have against us. Since we have been forgiven so much, we should in turn forgive. Forgiving or not forgiving others is an act of our own will. It's our choice. But to forgive others is imitating Christ. Jesus did it, Stephen did it, and you can do it!!! Question is, will you?

Father, thank You for this day and a life that no one can steal from us. Lord, open the windows of heaven and pour abundant blessings upon us and our family today. Lord, we trust that You have hidden our life with You and that we will share in Your glory when You come back. Lord, give us courage in the face of life's most difficult challenges to believe and anticipate sharing in Your glory. Lord, thank You for forgiving us of so much, and we ask You now to help us forgive others. Lord, use us to be a light that leads others to You.

Father, we love You. Amen.

NOTES

THE BLESSING

The Lord bless you and keep you; The Lord make His face shine upon you, and be gracious to you; the Lord lift up His countenance upon you, and give you peace.

Numbers 6:24–26, NKJV

God is for you. I can't think of a more powerful, more hopeful, more truthful statement to declare! We're never without hope. We can believe God for the next moment. We can trust Him for what we need. The circumstances around us might feel uncertain. But we can stand on the certainty that God is faithful. He's not surprised. He's not shaken. And He won't leave us or forsake us. That's what the blessing is about. It expresses the heart of God over us and then our responding to it and receiving it with an amen.

Friend, this is *the blessing* from God over us. He loves us. He is with us. He is for us. And in a season of such fear, loss, and disappointment, I'm so thankful we have the opportunity through these scriptures to declare truth into the atmospheres of our hearts, homes, and nations. These scriptures are the desire of God's heart for His people.

What more do we need? If God of the universe, the Creator of all things, is favorable toward us, then we need nothing more. God only wants the best for His children. His desire is to bless us. God's countenance is the expression on His face when He sees us, and it is a permanent smile. He is not disappointed or angry as some think. God is pleased with us regardless of what we do or don't do.

We are in Christ and no longer under the curse, and so we are in His eternal favor. God does not measure His love for us by our actions or words. He does not have a measuring stick that He pulls back when we mess up. We are in Jesus, and that is who He sees when He looks at us.

Remember that when Jesus was on the cross, the Father had to turn away from Him, because at that moment Jesus took our sin upon Him, which made Him sin. God, being a holy God could not look upon His own Son in that moment, and because of the sacrifice of Jesus on the cross, God's eye shifted from being on His Son to looking upon us in Christ Jesus.

We are His righteousness, and God's love focuses on us. He is delighted with His children and treats us with kindness and goodness. When God's face shines upon us, it is His favor and acceptance. Let's open our arms and tell God we receive His blessing!!!

Father, thank You for this day and for waking us up and setting us on our way. Lord, let Your abundant blessings flow like a river over us and our family today. Lord of every good and perfect gift, Your blessings are too many to count and too wonderful to fully comprehend. Lord, give us eyes to see and ears to hear so that we can share Your blessings with others today. Lord, use us to share the blessing of Your mercy and grace with others today.

Father, we love You. Amen.

NOTES

WATER OF LIFE

Jesus answered and said to her, "If you knew the gift of God, and who it is who says to you, 'Give Me a drink,' you would have asked Him, and He would have given you living water."

John 4:10, NKJV

In biblical times, where there was no water, there was no life. People died during droughts. Likewise, unless the living water of the Spirit is flowing in us, we and our churches will have an absence of spiritual life and little vitality. Just as in the desert, no water equals death, no growth, and no fruit.

We can attend church regularly and have perfect doctrine, but without the Holy Spirit to water us, we will wither and die. Jesus talked openly about the life-giving properties of the Spirit. "On the last and greatest day of the festival, Jesus stood and said in a loud voice, 'Let anyone who is thirsty come to me and drink. Whoever believes in me, as Scripture has said, rivers of living water will flow from within them'" (John 7:37–38, NIV). By "rivers of living water," Jesus was referring to the Spirit that believers would later receive.

When the Spirit of God comes, we have new life. Without the Spirit of God, we're left to struggle with our self-effort, which is riddled by moral weakness and sinful tendencies. But when the Spirit comes, we have joy, hope, and power. Notice that Jesus doesn't refer to a drop of water but to "rivers of living water." Like a river, the Spirit flows, a force of power that comes into us and then flows out so we can be a blessing to others.

God uses water as a symbol of the Holy Spirit in a slightly different way when He says, "I will be like the dew to Israel; he will blossom like a lily" (Hos. 14:5). We all have witnessed the grass and flowers glistening with tiny drops of refreshing water. By using this metaphor, God is saying He will be like the dew, which settles quietly in the night and coats the ground by morning.

Dew can't form when conditions are too hot or the wind is too strong. Likewise, we can't be refreshed by God when we're too busy running around. And the gift of God that the Lord Jesus spoke of to this woman at the well is His free gift of salvation, which is openly available to all who will accept God's gracious offer of redemption and be cleansed of their sin by faith in Christ.

Today, people who are spiritually dying of thirst will surround most of us. Will we take water to them? Oh, they don't understand their need, nor do they even know how to ask about it, but it is still so very deep. Do we care enough to change a small witness, a kind word, or a mention of His name? Jesus was very gracious and loving with this woman as He explained her need to her. We need to follow the lead of our Savior by gently and lovingly offering water to those in need today!!!

Father, thank You for this day and life-giving water of the Holy Spirit. Lord, open the storehouses of Your abundant blessings and let them fall upon us and our family today. Lord, thank You that You sought us out when we were dead in our sins and sinking deep into the miry pit of sin, self, selfishness, and seduction.

Lord, thank You that You are the living water, in whom alone are the words of eternal life and that in You we have been made new. Lord, may Your rivers of living water flow out through us to others who are in need of Your forgiveness today.

Father, we love You. Amen.

NOTES

NOTHING TO COMPARE

For I consider that the sufferings of this present time are not worthy to be compared with the glory which shall be revealed in us.

Romans 8:18, NKJV

The world in which we live is a fallen world, a place of suffering and trials and times of heartaches and problems, a life of difficulties and sickness, a season of disappointments and death. Afflictions and anguish stalk our path like a hungry pack of wolves, and they are no respecter of persons or position, clime or creed, wise or foolish, young or old, believer or non-believer.

And if this were all that life offered to humanity, we would indeed be the most miserable of species, for we would remain dead in trespasses and sins, without God and without any hope in the world. But this is a verse of contrasts. Suffering is placed alongside great glory, sadness is contrasted with lasting joy, despair is put in contradistinction with the glorious hope that is set before us while death is forever swallowed up in the abundance of everlasting life!!! GLORY!!!

It is no secret that some of our world's most empathetic, loving, and truly beautiful people are those who have known suffering, have experienced loss, and have lived through devastating defeat. God, as our loving Father, builds our character through discipline and love. This of course includes discomfort on our part, and sometimes our struggle is truly profound.

However, it is not without purpose. Suffering and all its aggressive associates pale into blinded insignificance when placed in their correct eternal perspective, for when laid alongside the truth of the gospel and the glory that shines forth from its eternal pages, they are not eve worthy to be considered in the same breath as our reality in Christ and our eternal heavenly future!!!

Father, thank You for this day and for Your wonderful words of wisdom in Scripture. Lord, let Your abundant blessings be our family's portion today. Lord, may we become so firmly grounded in the truth of Your Word and the glory that is revealed that we can place the sufferings of this present time in its correct perspective. Lord, give us the courage and boldness to face those challenges with the conviction that they are actually minor in comparison to the glory You will share with us when You return. Lord, use us to be the voice crying into a dark, decaying world, the life-giving gospel of Your grace.

Father, we love You. Amen.

NOTES

SALVATION STRENGTH

You pushed me violently, that I might fall, but the LORD helped me. The LORD is my strength and song, and He has become my salvation.

Psalm 118:13–14, NKJV

In verse thirteen we learn that the author was pushed hard to the point of falling. This wasn't merely an accidental nudge or a bump, but a violent action intended to knock the author over in order that he might not get up again. The enemies that surrounded him in the prior verses were seeking his destruction. Not only was he pushed by his enemies but also he was falling. If someone weaker than you pushes you, you can remain standing because you're stronger than they are.

This was not the case for the writer of this psalm! His enemies were overcoming him; they were pushing him hard, and he could not stand. He was helpless and falling. A glorious interruption happens amidst the difficulty: "But the LORD helped me." As the author was headed to his destruction, someone intervened. It was here in this place that the psalmist found God to be three specific things for him: his strength, his song, and his salvation.

Not many people want to go through hard times or be confronted with their own weakness, but it's in the place of our weakness, our discouragement, and inability to rescue ourselves, that we meet a God who is. In our weakness, He is strong. In our silence, He's our song. In our need, He is our salvation.

The truths of God are never meant to be distant theories we abstractly ponder in our ivory towers but rather truths that find us in real-life pits of despair and dark alleyways and lead us home again.

May we never settle for simply "knowing" that God is strong, but may His strength find us in our weakness. May we not simply hear about the joy of those rescued but also may God's song find a home in our hearts and mouths. May God's salvation not simply be a chapter in a systematic theology book we read but rather may we taste and see that God has become our salvation . . . not just once, but over and over and over again. May we never forget that our strength, song, and salvation have a face in Jesus. We were fallen and beyond repair; our enemy had a stranglehold on each and every one of us at our birth.

Jesus became weak so we might become strong. He cried out in agony on the cross that we might sing out in praise! He was led unto destruction so we might be led into God's salvation! And for this, may we will be eternally thankful!!!

Father, thank You for this day and Your amazing grace it holds. Lord, let Your abundant blessings flow over us and our family today. Lord, we thank You for Your wonderful love that is beyond our ability to know. Lord, give us Your wisdom and the strength of Your Spirit to make us what You want us to become. Lord, use us to carry out Your will in our lives and in so doing to help others in their journey to heaven as well. Lord, we ask a special prayer for our country and our leaders.

Father, we love You. Amen.

NOTES

DISCIPLINE FOR THE HEART

Apply your heart to instruction, and your ears to words of knowledge.

Proverbs 23:12, NKJV

This is a simple admonition here, yet if we will look at it carefully, it will yield to us some very helpful information. The first thing we see is that we are to apply our heart to discipline. The word "apply" here means "to bring to." Thus, God is saying that we need to bring our hearts to something. Here we read that what we bring our hearts to is discipline.

The word "discipline" translates from *musar,* which means to instruct with discipline. It refers most often to the discipline given by a father both by word and by the rod. It is very easy when discipline is applied to us for us to not allow it to reach the heart. We may hear the words and receive the correction, but we do not bring our hearts to it.

True correction and discipline is for the heart, not the bottom. It might be applied to the rear end with the rod, but the aim in these things needs to be directed to the heart. What Solomon is saying, though, is for the one receiving the discipline. Apply your heart to what God is trying to teach you. The second admonition here is that we also apply our ears to words of knowledge.

Knowledge here refers to more than just head learning. Solomon is telling us about knowing of God and His ways. He refers to a working knowledge, a practical knowledge, intimate knowledge, knowledge that truly changes the way we act. The verb "apply" is assumed here; thus; we are told to bring our ears to this knowledge that God is seeking to give us. It is listening to learn and to apply it to one's life.

This is key to our becoming wise. If we will truly bring our hearts and ears to what God is seeking to communicate to us, we will be blessed greatly. God longs for us to be wise and to know and follow Him with all our hearts.

These two practices, bringing our hearts to times of discipline, and bringing our ears to hear obediently what God says to us, will assure that we grow and personally experience all the godliness that God desires to give us when He works and speaks in our lives!!!

Father, thank You for this day and for setting us on our journey today. Lord, open up the windows of heaven and let Your abundant blessings pour out over us and our family today. Lord, we are grateful that You sent Your Word to guide us in the way that we should go. Lord, thank You for keeping us on the straight and narrow. Lord, we love Your Word. It is filled with life and faith. Lord, give us the desire to read and study it more diligently. Lord, open our understanding and give us revelation so we will be able to apply the truths found in it to our lives.

Lord, use us to boldly proclaim the Word of truth to all whom you bring into our path.

Father, we love You. Amen.

NOTES

THIRSTY?

On the last and greatest day of the festival, Jesus stood and said in a loud voice, "Let anyone who is thirsty come to me and drink. Whoever believes in me, as Scripture has said, rivers of living water will flow from within them."

John 7:37–38, NIV

Streams of living water for dying hopes, cool water for parched hearts, refreshing water for those tired and weary, of course, refers to much more than a liquid we can drink with our lips. This is the ultimate water of the soul that God longs to give to us, His children.

Let's spend today refreshing ourselves with the promises of Jesus and trusting that, as we draw close to Him, the Spirit will restore our souls. People have often tried to quench that inner void in their lives through various things, such as recreation, success, popularity, narcotics, and even religion. Jesus invites those who are thirsty to come to Him and drink.

By faith, we can receive Him as Savior and find the peace that He alone can provide. He then promises that He will place a spring of living water with those who truly belong to Him. This, of course, refers to the Holy Spirit who indwells in us as the children of God at the moment of our conversation.

The Holy Spirit from within provides the peace and fulfillment that we all need. This is the promise of God: rivers of living water flowing from within us. Jesus is able to satisfy the thirsty soul, but where are the thirsty souls?

Where are the souls that thirst for God, to know God in His fullness? Far too many are satisfied with their religion and no meaningful relationship with God. Even many who profess to be born again exhibit little desire for a closer walk with the Lord. It is safe to say that one reason we do not see more of a manifestation of God's grace and power working in our lives and churches is because of this lack of thirst or desire.

May God help us to maintain a thirst for Him and His glory in our lives and continue to trust Him for His grace and power to be manifest in and through us. This great promise is to him "that believes in me." To those who thirst for Him, and look to Him in utter dependence, He promises "rivers of living water." Drink with me from his bottomless well. You don't have to live with a dehydrated heart.

Father, thank You for this day and the living water of Your Word. Lord, pour out Your abundant blessings upon us and our family today. Lord, thank You for being the One who can quench our thirst. Lord, help us to draw from Your wisdom, strength, and Your presence within us. Lord, we come thirsty, and we come to drink and to receive. Lord, we receive Your work on the cross and in Your resurrection. Empowered by your Holy Spirit, we can do all things through Christ, who gives us strength. We receive Your Lordship. Lord, use us to bring others to the well of Your Word and drink from its abundance.

Father, we love You. Amen.

NOTES

COMFORTING OTHERS

Praise be to the God and Father of our Lord Jesus Christ, the Father of compassion and the God of all comfort, who comforts us in all our troubles, so that we can comfort those in any trouble with the comfort we ourselves receive from God.

2 Corinthians 1:3–4, NIV

When life is tiring, when we are struggling with our sin, when family members aren't saved, when bills aren't paid, when work is exhausting, when your health is falling, when your loved ones are hurt, when the future is unsure, and when a good friend leaves, it is easy to be discouraged.

Discouragement is a thief. It steals our vitality, our zeal, our joy, our peace, and our contentment. If discouragement dwells long with us, its friends will soon join. Their names are fatigue, hopelessness, despair, self-pity, depression, doubt, and bitterness. Sometimes, discouragement can be so strong that we even don't want to go on.

Discouragement is dissatisfaction with the past, distaste for the present, and distrust of the future. It is the result of blindness. It is ingratitude for the blessings of yesterday, indifference to the opportunities of today, and insecurity regarding strength for tomorrow. It is unawareness of the presence of God, unconcern for the needs of our fellow man, and unbelief in the promises of His Word.

If we have nothing to rely on, or we forget our blessing and look at our circumstances, then that is when discouragement begins to take hold. Instead, what we need is encouragement. We need hope and peace and the knowledge that the Lord knows our troubles, has great concern and compassion for us, and is not leaving us unloved or uncared for. Keeping your eyes on Jesus is the best way to be encouraged. In Him, you can have comfort and peace and encouragement. You need to find Him and His words, and by faith, rest in Him. Be encouraged because God is a God of mercy and comfort. Take encouragement because God is there in your afflictions. *You should be encouraged because you can be instruments of comfort to others.* Encouragement is something that belongs to us as a Christian.

We do not have to live in a world of hurt and doubt. We don't have to live alone. We don't have to weep in solitude. We have the body of Christ to lift us up. We have the Word of God to teach us. We have the Holy Spirit dwelling in us who warms our soul. We have the God of encouragement waiting to show us His mercy and love. But we need to trust. We need to remember the Lord's blessing. We need to depend on Him. We need to keep our eyes on Jesus and Him alone!!!

Father, thank You for this day and the breath of Your Word that guides our way. Lord, open the storehouses of Your abundant blessings and rain them down upon us and our family today. Lord, thank You for knowing our heart, caring about our concerns, and comforting us when we are wounded. Thank You, Lord, for all the comfort and grace that You have bestowed on us without measure. Bless the Lord of my soul and all that is within me bless His holy name. Lord, use us to share Your grace, mercy, and comfort with someone else today.

Father, we love You. Amen.

NOTES

REPENTANT HEART

"Now, therefore," says the Lord, "turn to Me with all your heart, with fasting, with weeping, and with mourning." So rend your heart, and not your garments; return to the Lord your God, for He is gracious and merciful, slow to anger, and of great kindness; and He relents from doing harm.

Joel 2:12–13, NKJV

There are many instances when there is a call for repentance. Here the prophet Joel is not only calling for the nation to turn away from sin but is also reminding them that God is faithful and that is why He is offering His hand of forgiveness toward them.

The reminder here is that despite our sin, God is faithful to forgive when we come to Him. Sin is always going to be something that Christians are going to struggle with. However it is not something that holds us captive anymore because Jesus's death on the cross covered our sin. Joel here is also reminding us that there is nothing we can offer that can cover our sin.

Jesus is asking for a true repentant heart that is open to His forgiveness and grace. It is a simple yet profound task for us to come to the realization that we are weak and in need of a loving Savior. Trust in His faithful and loving grace to lead and guide us to follow after Him each and every day.

We are no longer slaves to sin. Christ's work on the cross offers us a place in which we are able to come to Him with our sin, lay them before His feet, and accept His forgiveness. The "day of the Lord" was used by many prophets in the days of Israel. It was synonymous with the final judgment; the time when God would return and make all enemies His footstool and restore order in the world. Joel warns of this day soon to come.

Yet Joel also hints at possible grace for those who will turn from their ways and follow the Lord. This grace was demonstrated by God when He became flesh incarnate as Jesus. Rather than wiping out the earth, He gave us the greatest demonstration of love. The dreaded day of the Lord was postponed and replaced with an age of grace.

But do not be fooled into thinking that there will be no day of reckoning. There will be a return, and when that happens, Jesus will separate the sheep from the goats and cast away those who are evil. We will eventually face our Maker, either on the day of His return or when we pass from this life to the next. We must live with the conviction that we will indeed be judged and our behavior matters. The condition of our hearts is important. Do not be caught before the Lord unprepared to account for the life you've lived!!!

Father, thank You for this day and Your amazing mercy and grace to walk in it. Lord, let Your abundant blessings be our family's portion today. Lord, thank You for the book of Joel, which bears witness of Your goodness and grace to all who will trust in Your Word. Lord, we pray that You would help us to make our outward life a demonstration of a changed, inner life that trusts You implicitly, in thought, word, deed, and motive. Lord, grant to us, young and old alike, the wisdom to listen to You and to turn back from going our own way. Lord, use us to be the light of Your love to those whom You send our way.

Father, we love You. Amen.

NOTES

ON THE ROAD

And they said to one another, "Did not our heart burn within us while He talked with us on the road, and while He opened the Scriptures to us?"

Luke 24:32, NKJV

Do our hearts burn when Jesus speaks? Does it burn with conviction, but more often, does it burn as having been affected by a supernatural influence? Have we known a series of life-changing moments when the heavens opened, and all became clear?

On the very day that the tomb of Jesus was found empty by Mary Magdalene, two men walked from Jerusalem to Emmaus. Both were disciples of Jesus and in a deep discussion about the report that Jesus was alive. Incredulous, they couldn't imagine it was true. At that moment, Jesus appeared and walked with them, although they didn't recognize Him. He challenged their unbelief about the resurrection and began to remind them of Old Testament prophecies about the Messiah's life, death, and rise to glory. His words were so dynamic that when it was time to leave them, they begged Jesus to stay longer. Later, when He broke bread with them, their eyes were opened, and He disappeared from their sight. Then they had this conversation: "We should have known. Didn't our hearts burn within us as He walked with us?"

When Jesus speaks, His words are potent. I'm stunned. A bit dissociated, unable to connect with the mundane, sleepless nights due to the excitement I feel. Voraciously hungry for more. Convicted of my sin. More alive than I've ever been. Wordless to describe the experience. This is the aftereffect of hearing the Rabbi's voice. Like the old hymn, "He walks with me, and He talks with me, and He tells me I am His own."

Any given day could be an "Emmaus Road" day. There are seasons of revelation. Sometimes Jesus gives us an "open heaven" day, and other times He is silent. We must live off the memories of His last visit. But one thing is for sure, His words bring physical, emotional, and spiritual impact. King David knew it when he said: "My heart grew hot within me, while I meditated, the fire burned" (Ps. 39:3). What is the most important spiritual skill we can cultivate?

To hear the voice of God. If we live the breadth of our Christian life trying to model the principles of the Bible as if it were a self-help book, not only will it not be exciting, but it also won't sustain us when storms hit. We are to feast on true companionship. I'm praying that we will have a "burning moment" today, a supernatural appointment with the Spirit of God.

Let's set our hearts in listening mode. Do our hearts burn within us as we read His Word? Ask Jesus to walk with you and help you be a passionate witness for His sake!!!

Father, thank You for this day and the breath of Your Word that makes our hearts burn for You. Lord, open the floodgates of heaven, and let Your abundant blessings flow over us and our family. Risen Lord, thank You for walking with us each day and hosting us at Your table. Lord, rekindle our faith that

Your light may shine in us today. Lord, bring to mind scriptures today that You want us to have. Help us understand them, believe them, and to let them change our life. Walk with us today, Lord Jesus. Lord, use us to share the grace of the gospel to all who cross our path today.

Father, we love You. Amen.

NOTES

TRUE WISDOM

Behold, You desire truth in the inward parts, and in the hidden part You will make me to know wisdom.

Psalm 51:6, NKJV

Decisions, decisions, decisions. More and more our lives are filled with decisions. We're asked to make choices on just about everything. I am not afraid of decisions. They're a necessary part of life. But some decisions we make have both natural and spiritual consequences.

Did you know that every decision we make has a consequence? It does, and our decisions don't only affect just us but oftentimes affect others as well. True wisdom may bring material reward, but its value far exceeds earthly riches. To those who receive it, it opens a path to life and security and equips us for leadership and right conduct.

There are many benefits to true wisdom. True wisdom is priceless. True wisdom leads to life. True wisdom brings prosperity; true wisdom gives us security. God is the essence of truth, and this quality should be reflected in the character of His children. Falsehood is condemned in Scripture, but truth is praised and advocated.

God takes pleasure in truth and honesty, which are marks of an upright person. And truth originates from God. So true wisdom is the truth that is found in God. And fellowship and relationship with God are the starting points to receiving and understanding what is the truth.

What is it that God really looks for in our lives? First and foremost, it is not the external practices of religion, not necessarily churchgoing, or other religious acts. God looks much deeper than those. He looks right down into the innermost depths of our hearts and our lives. Elsewhere, the Bible tells us that God does not see as man sees, because man looks on the outward appearance, but God looks on the heart (1 Sam. 16:7).

If we come to that place, then we can say, like King David, "You teach me wisdom in the innermost place." There is a secret place in our innermost being where we can begin to hear the voice of God and learn from Him, and He teaches us wisdom there!!!

Father, thank You for this day and for waking us up and setting us on our journey through it. Lord, open the storehouses of heaven and pour out Your abundant blessings over us and our family today. Lord, thank You that You give us wisdom liberally. Lord, thank You that we can come to You in prayer and conversation to seek Your will and way for our lives. Lord, forgive us when we seek our own ways. Lord, guide and direct us in Your will, and help us stay on the path that You have given us to follow, and may You be glorified in everything we do today. Lord, use us to boldly proclaim Your gospel of grace to all today.

Father, we love You. Amen.

NOTES

KNOCK ON THE DOOR

Behold, I stand at the door and knock. If anyone hears My voice and opens the door, I will come in to him and dine with him, and he with Me.

Revelation 3:20, NKJV

An unexpected knock at the door from a dear friend or family member is a welcome surprise. Few occasions are as precious as seeing a long-absent loved one who comes to visit. "Here I am!" they say as you open your door, and their presence fills you with joy. Jesus stands at our door, knocking.

We may think sometimes that He is far removed from us and our church bodies, but He is, by His own revelation, as close as the door to our homes and our church communities. He wants us to hear His knocking; He is that close. And Jesus longs for us to do more! He wants us to respond and open all our closed doors in our life.

Maybe you are afraid to open the door of your life to Jesus. After all, how does one welcome the Son of God, the Almighty, into their whole life? Or maybe just having Jesus inside your heart is as close as you want Him to be. But Jesus keeps knocking, eager for us to open our lives to Him. He wants to be as close as a beloved friend in our lives.

Do not worry about how to welcome Jesus in. Just open the door. He promises to take care of the rest. He will come in and celebrate with whoever opens the door, bringing joy and abundance so your life will be filled with even more than the greatest feasting, fun, and goodness of life you could imagine.

Jesus doesn't knock on the doors of our hearts and lives so He can have a superficial, distant, one-way relationship with us whereby we are constantly looking over His shoulder at all life's distractions. Jesus is inviting us into an intimate relationship with Him through faith. He died and rose again so we can have a personal, forever relationship with God. He wants to sup with us and us with Him!!!

Father, thank You for this day and for Your unfailing love that sustains us through it. Lord, let Your abundant blessings be our and family's portion today. Lord, what a gift of love and honor You bring by knocking at our door. Lord, come in and transform us by Your presence. Lord, thank You for speaking to us through Your ministry and words. Lord, keep us from discarding Your request to allow You to enter our hearts, bring peace to our minds, and change our lives forever. Lord, use us to be the light in a dark world today.

Father, we love You. Amen.

NOTES

ABIDING

As the Father loved Me, I also have loved you; abide in My love. If you keep My commandments, you will abide in My love, just as I have kept My Father's commandments and abide in His love.

John 15:9–10, NKJV

Jesus is the eternal, uncreated Son of God who was in the bosom of the Father from before the foundation of the world and who has been loved by the Father from eternity past. The love that the Father has for the Son is deep, abiding, immeasurable, and eternal love. It is a love that passes the understanding of our limited human minds; it is a love that can never be comprehended by our understanding.

And yet on the eve of His crucifixion, Jesus told His disciples that the love He has for them is the same as the love that the Father has for His only begotten Son, and the Lord Jesus has that same depth of love for *all* of His children. He loves all who are called by His name with an everlasting love, for He told us that. "As the Father has loved Me, so I have loved you. Abide in My love."

We are accepted by the Father, in Christ, and we are loved with an incomprehensible love by the Lord Jesus Himself, who has called us to abide in His love. Let us abide in Him and rest in His love, so we may bear fruit, much fruit, to the praise and honor of our Father in heaven.

When Jesus asks us to obey, let's not see it as something onerous, burdensome, and limiting. Instead, let's see Jesus' command, and our obedience to that command, as the protection of a loving Savior trying to safeguard, bless, and care for His beloved children. When we obey Jesus, we remain under the protection of His love rather than in the danger of our rebellion!!!

Father, thank You for this day and the amazing, unfailing love You fill us with. Lord, open the windows of heaven, and let Your abundant blessings flow over us and our family today. Father, thank You that You loved us so much that You sent Your Son to die for us. Thank You, Lord Jesus, for Your immeasurable love toward us. Lord, we pray that we may keep Your commands and remain in Your love every moment of the day, just as You kept Your Father's commands and remained in His love. Lord, Your ways are not our ways; Your understanding is way beyond our understanding. Lord, use us to love others with the same love You have for them.

Father, we love You. Amen.

NOTES

PROFITABLE WORD

All scripture is God-breathed and is useful for teaching, rebuking, correcting and training in righteousness, so that the servant of God may be thoroughly equipped for every good work.

2 Timothy 3:16–17, NIV

The apostle Paul tells us in these verses that God's Word is good for us; it is profitable. He lists four functions of the Word of God in our lives: content, conviction, correction, and character. God left us His Word not simply to increase our knowledge but to infect our character and conduct. This enables us to see how important God's Word is to the very foundation of our lives.

The best way to assemble things is usually with instructions found in the box. The best way to build life is always on the instructions found in God's Word. Paul wanted to make sure both Timothy and we understand the inspiration and usefulness of Scripture in daily life. Paul noted that Scripture is inspired by God and therefore completely trustworthy. The complete contents of the Bible have God's stamp of approval.

The guidance of Paul and other godly figures in Timothy's life was secondary and supplemental to the authority of God's Word as the source of His revealed truth for His followers. Because Scripture is inspired by God, it is useful to His followers in many ways. Bible study is one of the main ways God speaks to us. It is the way we learn about God and His will for our lives. The Bible is beneficial for teaching, so it's beneficial for learning. Rebuke and correction make God's Word useful for avoiding future sin. Training in righteousness points us to Christ; we can't be righteous apart from Him.

The Bible, when actively read, engages us with God Himself. Thank God for His promise to thoroughly equip you for every good work as you engage with Him in His Word. Ask Him to help you meditate on His Word throughout the day, so that Scripture begins to come to mind and flow naturally in everyday conversations.

Let us *never* forget that *all* Scripture is God-breathed. From start to finish it is profitable, beneficial, enriching, and illuminating for all God's people. It teaches the truth, opens the way of salvation, warns of danger, and comforts us in our sorrows. It reproves us when we go astray, corrects us when we miss the mark, instructs us to do what is right, and is the most comprehensive training manual in righteousness!!!

Father, thank You for the beauty of this day and the breath of life found through Your Word. Lord, open the floodgates of heaven and allow Your abundant blessings to flow over us and our family today. Lord, thank You for the God-breathed Scriptures, Teach us, convict us, correct us, and train us through the living, powerful inspired Word of truth, that we may be equipped to carry out the work that You have ordained for us to do. Lord, please give us the character and the courage to put it into practical use. Lord, use us to share the gift of Your life-changing Word with all we meet today.

Father, we love You. Amen.

NOTES

TIRED AND BURDENED

Come to Me, all you who are labor and are heavy laden, and I will give you rest. Take My yoke upon you and learn from Me, for I am gentle and lowly in heart, and you will find rest for your souls. For My yoke is easy and My burden is light.

Matthew 11:28–30, NKJV

As we navigated the waters of COVID-19, social distancing and, yes, masks, and the emotional roller coaster of ever-moving targets of health and safety in our communities, there's one word I would use to describe my state of mind: "tired." Tired of the fear-driven state our country has been in for so long! I'm emotionally, physically, and even spiritually drained some days by it.

In these verses Jesus use the picture of farmers who would take an inexperienced ox and pair him with an older ox, and they would be "yoked" together as they pulled the plow side by side. This was so the older ox would set the pace for the younger ox, keep him on track, and teach him how to do the work properly. The older ox would do the heavy lifting until the younger figured out how to plow alongside him and become experienced, not going off course, or burning himself out before the work is finished.

In these verses Jesus calls us to be the younger ox, and He is the one setting the pace, keeping us on track and teaching us the work all the while doing the heavy lifting as we learn alongside Him. This is a beautiful picture of Jesus as He teaches us and trains us to do the work of ministry as we minister to our friends, family, coworkers, and neighbors.

If we are becoming overburdened, burnt out, or off course, we may have tried to take the lead away from Jesus, and in doing so, we bear the brunt of the work that Jesus is willing to take on for us. I would suggest that we haven't learned to come under Jesus as the mature, older ox. So if you're feeling burdened and heavy, as I have felt some days, I would remind you that Jesus is the one who sets the pace and keeps us on track. If we're feeling heavy, we aren't allowing the older ox to do His job and teach us, because if we did, the yoke would be easy and the burden would be light as we learn how to do the job correctly side by side with our Lord.

Let's lean not on our own understanding but allow Jesus to lead us in ways that refresh us and teach us and care for our soul. When we're yoked with Jesus, we move together with Him. We move in the same direction and at the same speed. And we move in the right direction and at the right speed. In need of rest for your weary soul today? Jesus is the answer!!!

Father, thank You for this day and Your strength to press on through it. Lord, let Your abundant blessings be our family's portion today. Lord, help us to face the challenges that we must confront. Lord, give us thankfulness for all that You have done to bless us. Lord, give us clarity to see that living for You is the best of all choices. Lord, thank You that You give us true rest for our soul and perfect peace in our heart—and that in the midst of any storm Your peace that passes all our understanding. Lord, give us the clarity to deal appropriately with those we meet today.

Father, we love You. Amen.

NOTES

BOLD LIVING

In the day when I cried out, You answered me,
and made me bold with strength in my soul.

Psalm 138:3, NKJV

The fruit of confident prayer is bold living! David developed a consistent history with the God of answered prayer. From his earliest days as a shepherd, David lived before the Lord in a life of prayer and worship. He experienced God's faithfulness when he prayed and knew the great strength of the Lord to give the victory. Because of this triumphant history with God, even in his youth David was transformed into a bold and stouthearted man.

Natural circumstances were not enough to cause him to shrink back because of this impartation of boldness that God had placed in his life through prayer. David displayed an absolute confidence in God as he boldly rushed in to confront Goliath in the faith of the Lord. He declared his victory before he even entered the battle, and then charged into the conflict in the strength of his history with God!

Are we developing a history in God? Are we gaining a rich experience of God's victory being displayed in our life as we pray and obey? The more we partner with God and see His power expressed both in and through us, the more that boldness will overtake us. The more we are transformed in our character so our conscience allows us to stand before God with confidence, the more we will have strength to stand against our enemies in the name of the Lord.

A confident life before God will always translate into a confident life before man in due time. Today, as we meditate on God's Word, let's turn our eyes to the possibilities that exist in God's answer. Let us consider and give way to hope in God. Let God make us into a bold representative of His name and His kingdom as we develop our life of faith!!!

Father thank You for this day and Your amazing grace and boldness to walk in it. Lord, open the storehouses of Your abundant blessings to pour out over us and our family today. Lord, what comfort and joy we gain from Your precious Word. Lord, we thank You that You are our strength and our shield. Lord, our hearts trust in You, and we praise and thank You for the help and comfort we receive through faith. Lord, thank You that Your ear is ever open to the cries of Your people. Lord, help us take every thought captive to You when circumstances arise that would otherwise overwhelm us and cause us to fear. Lord, Your joy is our strength; therefore, our hearts exult in grateful thanks and eternal praise. Lord, use us to be the light of Your love to those You bring our way today.

Father, we love You. Amen.

NOTES ______________________________

____

____

____

THE LEAST OF THESE

Then the righteous will answer Him, saying, "Lord, when did we see You hungry and feed You, or thirsty and give You a drink? When did we see You a stranger and take You in, or naked and clothe You? Or when did we see You sick, or in prison, and come to you?" and the King will answer and say to them, "Assuredly, I say to you, inasmuch as you did it to one of the least of these My brethren, you did it to Me."

Matthew 25:37–40, NKJV

I see him in the city day after day. His name is Louis, and he is homeless. His only means of transportation is a wheelchair. No matter how often I urge him to stay at our shelter, he refuses. The only thing he will do is accept prayer, some change, or some food. Some people would label him a loser.

In today's Scripture the Lord Jesus uses a different name to describe millions of people like Louis. He calls them "the least of these." The unborn child; the person who is mentally or physically challenged; people who are homeless, or hungry, or refugees; people in prison; and people who might never be able to live productive lives all are among "the least of these." And Jesus does not mean these are lesser people, as if they were not as important as others. He adds that whatever we do for someone in need, we do it for Him. As Mother Teresa put it, "When we look into the face of one of them, we see the face of Jesus." It's not up to us to judge people like

Louis who is homeless or anyone else who may face challenges or be at a disadvantage. Our task is simply to reach out and show them Jesus' love. While Jesus wants us to be compassionate and caring to all people, this passage is primarily about how we treat those the world seems to think are the least but whom Jesus values as His disciples.

The least, the last, and the left out become the primary ones who come to Jesus and find life, love, and lasting hope. Jesus' promise is that as we care for those in His community, no matter their circumstance, we are caring for Him. We can actually experience Immanuel, God with us, when we care for disciples of Jesus! Ask the Lord today to open your eyes to see His face in the faces of people who are down and out, disadvantaged, or challenged in other ways. And pray for a willingness to reach out!!!

Father, thank You for this day and the joy that fills our hearts because of Jesus. Lord, open the windows of heaven and shine down Your abundant blessings over us and our family today. Lord, give us a heart of concern and compassion for those who are left out and forgotten, especially those abandoned by the world who are Your disciples. Lord, give us courage to identify with those whom the world not only shuns and shames but also those the world persecutes and ridicules. Lord, give us a heart like You for the people who most depend upon You. Lord, use us to be someone's blessing today.

Father, we love You. Amen.

NOTES

WHERE, THEN, IS BOASTING?

Where, then, is boasting? It is excluded. Because of what law? The law that requires works? No, because of the law that requires faith. For we maintain that a person is justified by faith apart from the works of the law.

Romans 3:27–28, NIV

God is the source and giver of wisdom, and as led by the Holy Spirit, Paul argues logically and unquestionably that man is unrighteous, unprofitable, deceitful, destructive, and ungodly by nature. Our sin nature and the sins we commit have to be punished, and Jesus took the full and final punishment that we deserve, but it is only and exclusively and unalterably by faith in the death, burial, and resurrection of the Lord Jesus that we can be fully and forever forgiven of our sins and placed in eternal union with Christ, by which we are brought back into a right relationship with our heavenly Father.

And so Paul concludes this section of his clear and uncompromising presentation of the gospel of Christ by asking a simple rhetorical question, "Where, then, is boasting?" And immediately he gives the single, unalterable answer: "it is excluded." Boasting is excluded from our salvation. Meritorious works, kindly deeds, humanitarian actions, financial contributions, painful penance, and everything else by which man may contrive to secure his salvation is excluded, for the one and only way to God is by faith in the death, burial, and resurrection of Jesus Christ. Salvation is in Christ and Christ alone.

For we conclude that a man is justified by faith apart from works of law. Faith was credited to Abraham for righteousness, and by faith the men and women of Hebrews 11 were all made righteous in God's eyes, but it was all and only by faith. We too are saved by grace through faith in the finished work of Christ, as He has chosen us in Him before the foundation of the world that we should be holy and without blame before Him in love. "Where, then, is boasting? It is excluded." God forbid that I should boast save in the death of Christ my God.

God's salvation leaves us no room for boasting. We couldn't live up to the righteous demands of the law. When we were broken and sinful, God bought our salvation by sending Jesus and having Him pay the debt of our sin. We have nothing to boast about except the overwhelmingly generous grace of God and the incredible sacrificial love of our Savior!!!

Father, thank You for this day and the redemption we have in Your Son, Jesus. Lord, open the floodgates of heaven and shine down Your abundant blessings over us and our family today. Lord, thank You for redeeming us from the righteous judgment of the law. Lord, thank You for paying our debt for sin. Thank You, Holy Spirit, for cleansing us and making us holy. Thank You, God, for Your incredible grace found through

Jesus. Lord, use us to show Your amazing grace to all You bring our way today.

Father, we love You. Amen.

NOTES

JOYFUL NOISE

Make a joyful shout to the L*ORD, all you lands! Serve the* L*ORD with gladness; come before His presence with singing. Know that the* L*ORD, He is God; it is He who has made us, and not we ourselves; we are His people and the sheep of His pasture.*

Psalm 100:1–3, NKJV

Right out the gate the psalmist calls for a joyful noise to be made unto God. The psalmist's call is not merely to a small tribe or group of people but rather has the earth in view! No one is excluded. Not only is there a global call, but the psalmist qualifies this call by using the word "joyful." The sort of noise we make matters . . . it's not one of sadness, but one of joy. The word used here refers to a glad shout made in the presence of a king.

The whole earth has a singular almighty King who's not only worthy but also good to His people. He's no tyrant, but rather a joyful Ruler who invites us into His joy. Here the earth is called to serve the Lord with gladness. Again, the way we do something matters. God is not after heartless obedience but rather after hearts and lives that delight in Him.

The Lord has no regard for outward forms of worship if there be no inward adoration or if no devout affection be employed therein. Not only are we to serve Him but also sing to Him. Our glad service plays into our singing, and our singing plays into our glad service. No part of life is divorced from this worship of God! He is worthy.

In response to God and who we are in Him, how could we not make a joyful noise? How could we not serve Him with gladness or come into His presence with singing? Remember, no other recipe is acceptable for true praise and worship to the Father than what He has written in His Word. Let us shout GLORY!!!!

Father, thank You for this day and for the song of joy in our hearts. Lord, let Your abundant blessings flow mightily over us and our family today. Lord, we are truly thankful that You are God. Lord, thank You for being our Shepherd, our Father, and our Savior. Lord, empower us as we seek to display Your character and kindness to those around us. Lord, help us rejoice in You no matter what we face in life. Lord, use us to shine forth a life of grateful praise so others will see You and praise You today.

Father, we love You. Amen.

NOTES

ESTABLISHED STEPS

The steps of a good man are ordered by the LORD, and He delights in his way. Though he fall, he shall not be utterly cast down; for the LORD upholds him with His hand.

Psalm 37:23–24, NKJV

It is amazing to know that as a child of God, He directs, orders, and establishes our goings. That is, the Lord always leads us to the things that will cause us to glorify Him and will ultimately be for our good. This requires that we understand that He will always do what is best for us regardless of what it takes for us to either be corrected by chastisement or trials, which will produce strength and endurance in us.

It is necessary for each of us to fully accept that the Lord sovereignly controls our lives. He always knows what is best for us. We sometimes get beside ourselves and think that we know what is best, only to lead ourselves down a path to trouble. The Lord always knows how to get us back on track. The lives of God's children are precious to Him. He will direct our steps around danger, and He can protect us in the midst of danger. He omnipotently and omnisciently takes us through the course of life and guides us through the doom and disasters of life into His presence.

Our steps are ordered! God is calling us to realize that though we cannot see Him, God expects us to trust that He is working out His plan and purpose in our lives. He is sovereign and perfectly in control. The details here are important, and the more we notice God in all the details, the more we will trust Him moment by moment.

We will begin to notice His hand in everything in our lives. He is the master artist and author, always painting in the fine color and detail of God-ordained moments where He connects all the dots and writes new chapters in the story of life!!!

Father, thank You for this day and for guiding our steps through it. Lord, let Your abundant blessings be our family's portion today. Lord, thank You for Your faithfulness to us through all our faithful and unfaithful days, through all our obedience and disobedience. Lord, set our feet to stand firm in any uncertainties of this life. Lord, help us to believe that in the uncertainty of life, You are the God of certainty, and You are in control of everything. Lord, use us to be the blessing someone needs today.

Father, we love You. Amen.

NOTES

WALKING IN TRUTH

To the Jews who had believed him, Jesus said, "If you hold to my teaching, you are really my disciples. Then you will know the truth, and the truth will set you free."

John 8:31–32, NIV

To spot counterfeit currency, federal agents study the genuine bills rather than the fake ones. This practice makes any discrepancies in copies more noticeable. If we want to stand firm against deceit, we must learn to walk in truth. Jesus reminded His disciples in these scriptures that if they obey His Word, they are His disciples. The only way to obey Jesus' Word is to know what it is. The only way we will know truth is by knowing God's Word.

The more we study the Bible, the more we will recognize when someone says something that is contrary to Scripture. Studying Scripture takes time and discipline. Walking in truth is not easy. The world does not encourage believers to obey Jesus' teaching. However, the benefit of knowing Jesus' Word, the truth of our lives, far outweighs the cost. What practice can you set into place to help us walk in truth?

As we abide in His Word, it leads to a knowledge of this truth. This isn't a static knowledge, but rather this knowledge of the truth sets us free. Isn't that we ultimately desire? The truth is that every single one of us will be a disciple of something or someone; we will abide in and on something or someone's words.

However, there is only one whose Word can set us free, and His name is Jesus. Our culture today teaches us that to be free, we need to be true to ourselves, and that submitting ourselves to someone else's word brings about captivity and oppression. Yet here Jesus teaches us that as we abide in His Word, He leads us to truth and freedom. How is this possible? He is our Creator and knows the way we were made.

We were made to know God, to be in relationship with Him, and therefore learning from Him how we were made and how we are to relate to God is a roadmap to true freedom!!!

Father, thank You for this day and the Holy Spirit who gives us illumination and revelation. Lord, let Your abundant blessings be our family's portion today. Lord, thank You for the power of Your Word to guide us in all truth. Lord, we pray that You will help hide Your Word in our hearts. Lord, we pray that You will help us abide in You. Lord, we seek not only Your presence in our daily lives but also Your pleasure in the choices we make. Lord, please teach us more of Your truth as we pledge to live today in obedience to Your Word and Your will. Lord, use us to be the joy of Your love to those in our path today.

Father, we love You. Amen.

NOTES

BENEFITS

Bless the L*ORD, O my soul; and all that is within me, bless His holy name! Bless the* L*ORD, O my soul, and forget not all His benefits: who forgives all your iniquities, who heals all your diseases.*

Psalm 103:1–3, NKJV

Praising the Lord can be hard sometimes. Especially when you just don't "feel like it." So how do you motivate yourself to praise God even when you don't want to? One of the best ways to motivate yourself to praise God more is to remind yourself of how good He is. While heaven is our ultimate goal and our reason for living, we don't need to forget that God is with us *now.*

This life is far from heaven and is filled with all kinds of problems, disappointments, diseases, death, trials, sin, and heartaches. These are things that we all face at times and are just what we call a "normal" part of our lives. Of course, some face more than others and each of us may face different things, but we all have our share and then some. Paul tells us we can turn these things over to God in prayer with thanksgiving because the Lord is near.

When things get so bad that we don't even know how to express it to God in words, we have His Holy Spirit to intercede for us. When we think that surely God cannot really understand our plight, we are reminded that Jesus lived life just like we do, and He faced all these same things, and He understands. When life seems to turn against us, we can know that God will not allow us to be tempted beyond what we are able to bear with His help and His strength and will give us a way out of it. He never sleeps, gets distracted, goes on vacation, or ignores us. He is always ready to listen to our prayers and answer them.

So, we praise the Lord for this goodness to us. We praise His holy name because He continually blesses us, even in ways we don't seek or know. We cannot begin to know all God has done for us and how He has altered circumstances or given alternative opportunities. Praise God from whom all blessings flow, for our God is good and His love is everlasting. It can be easy to look at all the things going on wrong around you and have a bad attitude.

Decide today to do something different. Challenge yourself today to find some time to praise God, regardless of how you feel!!!

Father, thank You for this day and the praise You have put into our hearts today. Lord, open the storehouses of Your abundant blessings and let them flow over us and our family today. Lord, we do thank you for all you do for us every day. Lord, we praise You for the wisdom you give, and we seek it more. Lord, we praise You for your gift of creation, and we praise You for those who shared the gospel of Your grace with us. Lord, thank You for the strength You provide in times of trials. Lord, give us a pure heart so we will live in such a way that brings glory to You at all times. Lord, use us to help show others how to serve You and live for You.

Father, we love You. Amen.

NOTES

TRANSFORMED

Do not conform to the pattern of this world, but be transformed by the renewing of your mind. Then you will be able to test and approve what God's will is—his good, pleasing and perfect will.

Romans 12:2, NIV

If we want to have lasting change in our life, we need to refocus our mind. Specifically, we need to change our thought patterns away from what we don't want to focus on and toward what we do want to focus on. Because whatever we focus on is what we move toward.

Today's verse gives us the blueprint to change our thought patterns: "Do not conform." How often do we let other people shape our lives? God doesn't want us to be like someone else; He wants us to be the person He made us to be. So don't conform. Don't try to be like anybody else . . . the pattern of this world. "Pattern" means the model of everything we have learned in life. If we want to change, we have to change our pattern or model of living that we learned in our life. We need to replace the old, unhealthy pattern with a new one modeled after the life of Christ.

"Be transformed by the renewing of your mind" means that you are going to have to do some putting off and you are going to have to do some putting on. It's just like trying on clothes in a department store. Before you can try on the new stuff, you have to take off the old stuff. We're going to have to let go of the old attitudes, the old thought patterns, the old images that we've been living with, so we can put on the new garments God has for us.

As the old hymn says, "Have thine own way, Lord . . . mold me and make me after thy will!" Let's gladly offer Him our heart, our life, and our future to use for His glory!!!

Father, thank You for this day and for Your life-changing Word. Lord, open the windows of heaven and shine down Your abundant blessings upon us and our family today. Lord, help us to take captive all thoughts that are not from You. Lord, help us to hunger for Your knowledge and wisdom, to fill our minds with Your Word and Your love. Our hearts belong only to You, Lord. Lord, thank You for Your direction and guidance to enable us to live a better life through You. Lord, use us to be a bold witness of Your mercy, grace, peace, and joy to those we meet today.

Father, we love You. Amen.

NOTES

FOR GOD'S GLORY

Hear this, all peoples; give ear, all inhabitants of the world, both low and high, rich and poor together. My mouth shall speak wisdom, and the meditation of my heart shall give understanding.

Psalm 49:1–3, NKJV

Wisdom is something that can truly dictate the heart of one's life and actions. If one chooses to incline their heart toward things that are of more value and meaning, rather than material things that are only temporary, then one can truly say that their life is purposeful.

Living a life for God and not for our own pleasures helps us view life's good and bad through a more eternal perspective. What that means is we set our sight on knowing that one day we will be spending eternity with God and that all that we accomplished in this life that was not for God's glory will be meaningless and pass away.

Our hope ought to be set on looking forward to the day when we can leave all of this behind and spend our lives loving and worshiping God. Echoing the wisdom found in God's statutes, the psalmist highlights the fact that those who seek their identity in money or worldly things all have the same fate as the poor and even animals. The psalmist also says that no amount of money can ransom a life from the Lord.

We will never be able to escape the fate and the will of the Lord, no matter how much power and clout one gains here on the earth. We are all still mortals, and we will all one day meet our Maker. May we be always trying to live a life that will build up the kingdom of God and not the kingdom of self. We should not be impressed with the riches of men. When you set God's currency next to the rich man's millions, you know that only God can buy your soul from the clutches of eternal death.

This psalm produces in us a confident rejoicing in God and the certainty of the resurrection. We should also enjoy our freedom from the clutches of the idolatry of materialism. This psalm is an ideal exhortation for our modern world, where most people live in the lap of luxury. Yet it is intended for every person who has ever lived in this world, rich and poor alike. For it establishes what is really of value in this world. In a world of millions of books and billions of opinions, only the Bible gives us the truth, the nuggets of gold hidden in the dark corners of caves. These nuggets are well worth the effort of excavation. Riches won't buy you heaven, but God will!!!

Father, thank You for this day and Your amazing grace. Lord, let Your abundant blessing flow like a river over us and our family today. Lord, have mercy on us, "take our minds and think through them, take our lips and speak through them, take our hearts and set them on fire. Lord, we thank You for these Scriptures; they remind us our earthly wealth is only for this earth. It isn't eternal and we can't take it with us. Neither can we redeem our souls with our riches. Thank you, Jesus, for paying the ransom for our souls. Lord, help us to get the right perspective on life and build our lives more on things that are eternal. Lord, use us to be the touch of Your love to those You bring our way today.

Father, we love You. Amen.

NOTES

SEASONED SPEECH

Walk in wisdom toward those who are outside, redeeming the time. Let your speech always be with grace, seasoned with salt, that you may know how you ought to answer each one.

Colossians 4:5–6, NKJV

In this text we are reminded what our speech is to be like when speaking to nonbelievers and believers. As the people of God, when we open our mouth, we should be speaking words that are seasoned with the salt of God's grace.

In other words, there should be evidence of God's grace and His influence upon our hearts through the words that flow out of our mouth. Yes, what we speak should not only be pleasant, but it should also reflect who we are in God as the salt of the earth. When we were unsaved and separated from God, we spoke what we wanted, when we wanted, and how we wanted. Not so now that we have been born again by God's grace.

In these perilous times in which we live, we need God's wisdom as we go out with the gospel to evangelize to those who are lost. Indeed, our words must be seasoned with God's grace and divine wisdom. People of God, we must choose carefully the words we speak and always be ready to give an answer to anyone who asks. In our time when social media echoes with mean-spirited, ugly, and divisive words, we must hear the Lord's warning about choosing our words carefully.

Paul challenged us to be even more vigilant about what we say and how we say it. The apostle emphasized how significant our influence is on those who don't know Christ. We want to seize every opportunity to open the hearts of unbelievers to Jesus. The eternal destiny of those around may be resting on our conversations with them.

Let's season our speech with care. Let's take advantage of every opportunity we have to open the hearts of others to the grace of Jesus!

Father, thank You for this day and the breath of Your Word that sustains us. Lord, open the floodgates of heaven and flood Your abundant blessings over us and our family today. Lord, please help us to seek to display a winsome attitude with all people, but especially toward those who do not yet know you as their Lord and Savior. Lord, thank You for pouring out every single drop of grace at Calvary for us. Lord, may Your grace be what pours out of us. Lord, use our words to be the salt and light of Your words for others to feast on and find eternal life.

Father, we love You. Amen.

NOTES

PRIZED GOAL

I press on toward the goal to win the prize for which God has called me heavenward in Christ Jesus. All of us, then, who are mature should take such a view of things. And if on some point you think differently, that too God will make clear to you. Only let us live up to what we have already attained.

Philippians 3:14–16, NIV

Once we have trusted the Lord Jesus as Savior, we embark on a race through life to the finishing post. After a person has been born again, they are to grow in grace and in the knowledge of the Lord Jesus Christ. Once we are justified and placed in the family of God, we are called by our Father to sanctification, which is a lifelong process, in which we press on toward the goal of our heavenly calling, so we may gain the prize of the upward call of God in Christ Jesus. Each believer is called to run the race that God has set before them.

Every Christian has a specific purpose that God Himself has called them to achieve. Each has their own unique goal to attain, and that goal is purposeful and planned by the Father, for it is God who works in each of His children both to will and to do that which pleases God.

No two life journeys are the same, for we all face our own particular problems, disappointments, and challenges, and we are all equipped with our own unique God-given abilities, gifts, and graces. But the call of God for all His children is a life that is being conformed into the image and likeness of the Lord Jesus, Who is seeking us and the life which we now live in the flesh we live by faith in the Son of God, who loved us and gave Himself for us.

Let's use So challenge yourself today to not let go of the dreams and callings that God has placed on the inside of you. They might not always come to pass right away, but if you keep making steps toward them, they will come to pass in your life. Let us run the race that is set before us and press on toward the goal of the upward call of God—looking unto Jesus, the author and finisher of our faith!!!

Father, thank You for this day and the breath of life found in Your Word. Lord, open the storehouses of heaven and pour out Your abundant blessings upon us and our family today. Lord, we thank You that we are Your children. Lord, we want to live our lives the way that You have ordained, and run the race that You have set before us. Lord, help us to press on toward the goal of our calling in Christ Jesus, trusting in Him to overcome every problem, disappointment, and challenge we may face, to Your praise and glory. Lord, use us to be the blessing of Your love to those You bring our way today.

Father, we love You. Amen.

NOTES ______________________________

COMPLETE DEVOTION

Then Mary took a pound of very costly oil of spikenard, anointed the feet of Jesus, and wiped His feet with her hair. And the house was filled with the fragrance of the oil.

John 12:3, NKJV

Mary is a picture of pure, undistracted, and complete devotion to Jesus. With perfect vision she sees the glory, power, and beauty of Jesus. And because of her clarity of heart and mind, she holds nothing back in showing her love and devotion to Him.

Is our heart filled with the same love for Jesus that we are willing to do the same? Mary's offering of love was costly. It was extravagant. Judas accused her of excessive devotion to Jesus! Yet to this criticism Jesus responded, "Leave her alone." He knew that her offering of love came from a heart that was on fire with love for God.

It was a heart that saw the unsurpassed beauty of Christ and could not help but offer complete devotion in response. In an act of worship, Mary poured her perfume on Jesus' feet. She knelt to the ground and washed His feet, ignoring the opinions of others. Mary gave radically. She did not know if she'd be able to live through the day but trusted Jesus anyway. She gave with such extravagance that the disciples told her she'd given too much.

To put Mary's situation in today's terms, it would be like going to church this Sunday, feeling called to give, and writing a check for your entire year's salary! Yet, this is the same way God gave to us. He gave His best when He gave us Jesus. God not only calls us to radical faith, but He also calls us to radical giving.

May the same be true of us today! Let us serve the Lord faithfully and selflessly, but never as a distraction or replacement for our primary devotion to Him. Spend time today reflecting upon the worthiness and wonder of Jesus, and let your heart be renewed with praise and gratitude. Then, from that place of love, go forth to love and serve others as a pure offering of praise and thanksgiving.

When we truly know that Jesus loves us and that He ransoms those we love from death, how can we not be extravagant in our display of love for Jesus? Let's be like Mary who was more concerned to display her love extravagantly for Jesus and less concerned about the criticism of those around her. Will we be willing to worship Jesus with all we have and all that we are, no matter what others are saying?

Father, thank You for this day and the breath of life found through Your Word. Lord, open the floodgates of heaven and rain down Your abundant blessings upon us and our family today. Lord, we confess that way too often our display of love for Jesus is passionless and predictable. Lord, we truly love and appreciate You for Your unbelievable sacrifice and the victory over death that you purchased for us by Your agony. Lord, help us to be less concerned about criticism from others and freer to show our love for You. Lord, may we sit at Your feet and worship You with all that we are and all that we have. Lord, use us to serve You and love others extravagantly today.

Father, we love You. Amen.

NOTES

WORK OF GOD

Then they said to Him, "What shall we do, that we may work the works of God?" Jesus answered and said to them, "This is the work of God, that you believe in Him whom He sent."

John 6:28–29, NKJV

Have you ever had someone ask you what your life's work is, or what type of work you would like to spend the rest of your life doing? That can be a difficult question, especially today, when the average worker will have had ten to fourteen jobs. We quickly move from task to task, even job to job, and oftentimes there is little sense of continuity. Jesus gives us some great insight on what our answer should be while we are here on the earth. Jesus' answer to the question, "What must we do, to be doing the works of God?" is still the same in this age of rapid change:

"Believe in Him whom He sent." So the primary, overarching work of our life is believing Him, Jesus Christ, and walking as He walked. That is our daily agenda. So no matter what job you find yourself in, you still have your life's work at hand, believing in Him who was sent. We define each other in large measure by the work we do. God, however, defines us by His grace.

So the work God has for us, the way He wants us to "make our living," so to speak, is by fully trusting in Jesus. This is the orientation point for each of our lives! As believers, we have the life of Christ within us and the good works that God has prepared for us to do are to be accomplished in our new Christ-life and through the power of the Holy Spirit.

The works God has prepared for us to do cannot be achieved through the power we exert from our old self-life. As believers, we have to trust Him to work the works of God in us to believe that He does it and not us. We must not only believe in Him whom God has sent for salvation, but we have also to believe in Him whom God has sent day by day, to do His good works, in us!!!

Father, thank You for this day and for waking us up and setting us on our journey. Lord, open the windows of heaven and shine down Your abundant blessings upon us and our family today. Lord, we have trusted You as our Savior. Help us to continue trusting You for every step that we take in our life. Lord, help us to believe in You who the Father sent, for it is only through the power of Your Spirit that we can do the works that God has prepared for us to do. Lord, use us to share the gospel of Your saving grace to those You bring our way today.

Father, we love You. Amen.

NOTES

SHARPENED

As iron sharpens iron, so a man sharpens the countenance of his friend.

Proverbs 27:17, NKJV

I have found that there is a great benefit for the believer who surrounds themselves with those who are spiritually intelligent; those who show great wisdom in not only knowing the Scriptures but also have experience in living according to the Scriptures.

It is good to have those in our lives, who will cause us to become excited about the things of God. The individuals who are able to motivate us to not only know what the Scripture says but also to seek to live diligently in order to please the Lord, are a tremendous benefit. We too should seek to be that iron in the lives of others that is the sharpening influence that will bring about spiritual wisdom and spiritual intelligence in them.

There is a great advantage to the believer who desires to become better in their living in a world of relativism. There are those who can be the motivating factor that pushes us to be better spiritually than where we currently are right now. That's why it is so important for each of us to build growing relationships with others in life. We all need people who can help us rub off the hard edges and who honestly have our best interests in mind when they do it.

There are times when these sharpening conversations, even from loving friends, can come across as harsh, mean, or judgmental. But it definitely helps to know that these people care and that they have a genuine interest in helping us improve. Growing as a Christian is important. Choosing friends who will sharpen us is one practical way we can grow. God designed us to need each other for fellowship and for advancing His kingdom here on earth!!!

Father, thank You for this day and the blessing of those who love You with all their hearts, minds, and souls who sow into our lives. Lord, let Your abundant blessings flow from the storehouses over us and our family today. Lord, You are holy, awesome, and worthy of all our praise. Lord, we ask that You send people into our life that will encourage us in our faith. Lord, help us to have a teachable spirit, so we can continue to grow in You. Lord, You are the source of all strength and goodness. Lord, thank You for helping us to grow in faith and for putting friends in our life, who can help sharpen us. Lord, use us to sharpen those whom You put in our lives.

Father, we love You. Amen.

NOTES

COME BOLDLY

Let us therefore come boldly to the throne of grace, that we may obtain mercy and find grace to help in time of need.

Hebrews 4:16, NKJV

Life can be filled with all kinds of dilemmas that can leave us in a state of confusion and despair. We are often hit with disappointments in life that can be very debilitating. When we are hit with intense adversity in this life, it is so comforting to know that our great High Priest endured pain and despair just as we do.

Therefore, we are able to confidently approach God's throne of grace where we can receive the strength we need to keep moving forward. It is impossible to try to make it through this life without the grace that God provides for us in order to make it. We are helpless, and when we rely on our own ability to pull ourselves through, we will ultimately fail.

We often hear clichés that tell us to "pull ourselves up by our bootstraps." Nowhere in Scripture does God tell us to do that. He tells us to trust in Him with all our hearts. He then provides the grace we need in our weaknesses. Be strengthened and encouraged in Christ. The call today is to draw near to the throne of God in prayer with confidence and assurance, so that we may find the help we need. People of God, we must daily remind ourselves of this one thing: our God is "God of the impossible." *Nothing* is too hard for Him.

The Lord our God is declaring to us today that He is our help in our time of need; therefore, *if* we come, we are promised to find grace and mercy at His throne. Searching for peace in a world full of chaos and confusion? Come boldly to God's throne of grace. Searching for love and hope? Come boldly to God's throne of grace in prayer.

When we suffer, the enemy of our mind often comes to us with thoughts that are contrary to God's Word in his attempt to convince us that God doesn't care about us and that is why we suffer and He will not answer us, so we should stop wasting our time with these worthless prayers. The devil is a liar! Keep praying ! Trust God! At God's appointed time, He will answer! He promised us in this text that when we come in prayer, we will find the grace and mercy we need. Keep praying, people of God!!!

Father, thank You for this day and the blessing of mercy and grace when we need it. Lord, open the floodgates of Your abundant blessings, let them flood over us and our family today. Lord, help us to come boldly unto Your throne of grace daily. Lord, we receive your mercy and grace for every area of our life. Lord, help us to realize that You are there and ready to help us out with anything we need in accordance with Your will. Lord, help us to take comfort in the fact that we've got grace to help us in our time of need. Lord, use us to be the touch of Your mercy and grace to all we meet today.

Father, we love You. Amen.

NOTES

SPIRITUAL MATURITY

Anyone who lives on milk, being still an infant, is not acquainted with the teaching about righteousness. But solid food is for the mature, who by constant use have trained themselves to distinguish good from evil.

Hebrews 5:13–14, NIV

Once we are saved by grace through faith, we are to live by faith; to walk by faith; to mature in the faith and to grow in grace. We are to progress from spiritual infancy to spiritual maturity and to become disciples of Christ, students of the Scriptures and skilled in the Word of righteousness.

As believers who have trusted Christ for our salvation, we are to develop in our Christian walk and advance from simply taking in the pure milk of the Word to feeding on the strong meat of everything that proceeds from the mouth of God. We are to walk each day in spirit and truth as we regularly read, mark, learn, study, inwardly digest and practice the truth that we have been taught from the Word of God, so that our senses are trained to discern good and evil.

But we are to be nourished on the Word of God, and to practice biblical precepts and scriptural principles if we are to become spiritually disciplined mature believers. To do so means that we are to die to self and look to Christ alone. It requires that God's Word dwells in us richly day by day and that we are quick to eschew evil and do that which is good. We are to walk in spirit and truth, abide in Christ and He in us, so that in the power of the Holy Spirit we may bring forth much spiritual fruit to the glory of God.

As maturing Christians, we should desire an increasingly intimate relationship with our Lord and set our hearts on things above and not on the things of this earth. We are to remember that we are in Christ and that in Him, we died to our old sinful past, and our life is now hidden with Christ in God. We are to rejoice that Christ is our life. We are to pray without ceasing and in everything give thanks. And we are to remember that He is coming one day to take us to be with Himself, and that the day is fast approaching when we also will appear with Him in glory. Praise His holy name!!!

Father, thank You for this day and the breath of Your Word that sustains us. Lord, let your abundant blessings be our family's portion today. Lord, we pray that we continue to grow in grace and become spiritually mature. Lord, we pray that as we submit to the work of the Holy Spirit in our life that we may become increasingly like You, and that we live and work to Your praise and glory. Lord, these words have searched us, have found us out, have made us to see ourselves. We thank You for that. Lord, use us to be the embrace of Your love to those who need it today.

Father, we love You. Amen.

NOTES ______________________________

____

____

PURE HEART

Create in me a clean heart, O God, and
renew a steadfast spirit within me.

Psalm 51:10, NKJV

The sacrifices of God are a broken spirit, a broken and
a contrite heart—these, O God, You will not despise.

Psalm 51:17, NKJV

Why does God have to *create* a clean heart in us? Because it doesn't come naturally! We were not born with a clean heart. *Merriam-Webster Dictionary* primarily defines the word "create" as "to create into existence." This pure heart was something that did not exist! God must create it, and what's more, He must continually re-create it, because we can do nothing to either create it or maintain it in our own power.

All we can do is ask Him for that clean heart. Our need for a clean heart is so undervalued by today's lukewarm Christians. When your heart is pure and known sins are confessed, there are no roadblocks to fellowship with God through His Holy Spirit. You'll be open to His leading and blessing, as well as His hand on your shoulder, stopping you from misplacing your priorities and being deceived by your own heart.

If you read the rest of Psalm 51, David speaks of what he will be able to do when his heart is pure before the Lord. He'll be able to be an example and testimony to unbelievers. His heart will be free to rejoice and sing before the Lord. He will be able to enjoy renewed closeness with God from the place of repentance and redemption. It stands to reason that the flipside is also true. We are not able to do those things when our hearts are not clean.

My prayer for us today, as a fellow believer desiring to serve the Lord, is that we will come to the realization that David did. A clean heart must be brought about from scratch by God, and all we can do is desire it and ask for it. Do you deserve it? Let me caution you that the process won't be pretty. Sins may come to light under the illuminating torch of the Holy Spirit we invited in, sins that we might very well rather have never had seen the light of day. It won't be pretty or pleasant to experience, because all sin is ultimately ugly and unpleasant in the end.

I'm so thankful we can cling to the final phrase of verse seventeen: "A broken and contrite heart—these, O God, You will not despise." The unclean, impure heart invites judgment. But the repentant heart is always—ALWAYS—received with compassion and mercy and replaced with a clean one! Take a moment from what you are doing and let God's grace take hold of your heart. What a loving Father we have!!!

Father, thank You for this day and Your amazing grace to walk in it. Lord, open the windows of heaven and rain down Your abundant blessings upon us and our family today. Lord, help us be quick to realize when our heart isn't clean. Lord, help us be even quicker to admit we cannot cleanse it on our own and to ask You to recreate it. Lord, renew a right spirit within us so we may be a testimony of Your grace, sing without being strangled by our sin, and live the abundant life for which You have called and redeemed us. Lord, use us for Your glory and to the good of others around us.

Father, we love You. Amen.

NOTES

SEEK AND SEARCH

So that you incline your ear to wisdom, and apply your heart to understanding.

Proverbs 2:2, NKJV

For the L*ORD gives wisdom; from His mouth come knowledge and understanding; he stores up sound wisdom for the upright; He is a shield to those who walk uprightly.*

Proverbs 2:6–7, NKJV

There is only one source of wisdom. To look anywhere else is foolish and wasteful. All wisdom is from the LORD. And He gives it to whomever He will. Knowledge and understanding are also His gifts, and He speaks them by His Spirit, His Word, and preachers.

Wisdom, knowledge, and understanding are related aspects of the ability to judge rightly, to know the right moral or practical solution for unique dilemmas or situations. They are the means by which you can identify truth and error, right and wrong, good and evil. They are the conditions for a blessed and successful life of peace and righteousness. Wisdom is not measured by IQ, degrees, or achievements.

Wisdom is superior to these. Human intelligence is not a source of wisdom. A humble laborer of modest intelligence who fears and obeys God will have greater wisdom than a proud genius trusting his analytical but depraved mind. For the Lord gives wisdom!

Wisdom and character are worth more than intelligence. Human education is not a source of wisdom. Education can be a handicap. For the Lord gives wisdom! One sees God in every aspect of his simple life; another hallucinates about big bang theories and his monkey mother. God has declared war against this approach to wisdom. In verse six we see that God is the one who gives us godly wisdom, and it comes from His mouth and His understanding.

This means that if we want to be wise, we must read the Bible, as it records the things that He has spoken. As we read God's Word, we will receive His knowledge and understanding about any issue that we desire to know about. This means when we have a certain problem that we are dealing with in our lives, we should do two things immediately: 1) seek God in prayer about the problem, and 2) search the Bible as to what it says about the problem!!!

Father, thank You for this day and for waking us up and setting us on our way. Lord, pour out Your abundant blessings upon us and our family today. Lord, we are grateful that You have left us the Bible with all of its wisdom and knowledge, so that we do not get lost in this life or overwhelmed by the problems that we face. Lord, we thank You for every problem we face and for the help as we find the answer to overcome the situation. Lord, give us the grace to do that. Lord, use us to share the gospel of grace to all we meet today.

Father, we love You. Amen.

NOTES

SATISFIED SOUL

As the deer pants for the water brooks, so pants my soul for You, O God. My soul thirsts for God, for the living God. When shall I come and appear before God?

Psalm 42:1–2, NKJV

This is a wonderful illustration of one who was experiencing a terrible drought in his life. His soul was hurting, and his most ardent desire was for the realization of the presence of God in His life. He would not be satisfied until he searched every place until he experienced God's presence.

When we are searching for the knowledge of God's presence, it is then that we realize how much we love and need Him to quench our spiritual thirst. When one who has experienced God's dealings in their life is in a place where they do not realize that God is there; it can be a very hard time.

The psalmist paints the picture of a thirsty deer moving along the mountainside, intensely searching for much needed water in order to quench its thirst. The thirsty soul of one passionately searching to have their soul quenched by the living God will not be content until they experience God's satisfying presence in their life. It is important to know that when God's presence in our lives is our most precious desire, He is faithful to the utmost to quench our most intense yearning.

True health as a human being can only come by being obsessed with God. God must be the center of our lives.

Everything must revolve around our relationship with God for us to be healthy. In fact, balance is only found by having God at the center. Just as a deer would get sick and eventually die if it let chasing butterflies get in the way of finding water, there is nothing more important in life than thirsting for God and having that thirst met. Anything less is substituting a false cure, an idol, in place of God.

Our very souls are longing for God, but in our sinfulness, we let other things compete with God and we suffer in the process. True health and true balance, things we long for, come through total, laser-focused obsession for and devotion to God through Jesus Christ!!!

Father, thank You for this day and the breath of life we find in the water of Your Word. Lord, open the storehouses of Your abundant blessings to the fall upon us and our family today. Lord, hear our deepest longings for You and quiet our troubled souls with Your holy presence. Lord, we want to follow You because You are truth, because it is right, and that's who we are meant to be: Yours. Lord, we long for You, we need You, and You are life. Lord, help us to remember that there really is no distance between us but that You are always there. Lord, use us to be the living example of Your Word that others see today.

Father, we love You. Amen.

NOTES ______________________________

REST IN GOD

Thus the heavens and the earth were completed in all their vast array. By the seventh day God had finished the work he had been doing; so on the seventh day he rested from all His work. Then God blessed the seventh day and made it holy, because on it he rested from all the work of creating that he had done.

Genesis 2:1–3, NIV

Never has more work been accomplished in six days. The universe went from vast nothingness and emptiness to what it is as we know it by a few words of God in only six, twenty-four-hour days. Then God looked out at all that He had created and realized that it was "very good." So God rested. God wasn't tired though. He didn't need to take a break in His recliner and eat Doritos while watching college football for a while. He rested in that He simply stopped His work of creating.

But God was setting a precedent for rest to be carried forward until He would bring an end to the universe He made. With this Sabbath that the Lord took and with the seventh day of Sabbath that He ordained, God was establishing the extreme importance of rest. Weekends are a great time that Americans love to rest on. People head to the beach. They grill burgers and hot dogs. They enjoy a relaxing day with family or friends away from work.

Physical rest is a very important thing. God does want us to take care of our physical health and mental sanity. At the same time, there is rest that is much more important. The Sabbath that God took on the seventh day also points to the eternal Sabbath that all people will enjoy in the paradise of heaven. And as God ordained Sabbath for all people, God was also establishing the importance of spiritual Sabbath.

In worship, in devotions, in Bible study, and most specifically in our Savior Jesus, we find spiritual Sabbath. In Him we find rest for our souls. In Him, we find a Savior who gives us eternal rest for our souls. As we enjoy our days, we can remember the benefit of rest for our bodies. Yet, we can be reminded of the necessity of spiritual rest for our souls on a regular, daily basis. Finally, on every day we can look forward to the eternal paradise of heaven where both body and soul will rest forever.

Father, thank You for this day and for the Word of life that sustains us. Lord, open the floodgates of heaven and pour out Your abundant blessings over us and our family today. Lord, give rest to our weary soul each and every day. Lord, refresh and renew us with Your Word. Lord, guide us through this life until we rest with You forever in heaven. Lord, we believe that it's Your will for us to enjoy our work, so teach us how to do that. Lord, thank You for enabling us to earn a good living. Lord, use us to be the peace of Your love to those we encounter today.

Father, we love You. Amen.

NOTES

SHIELDED WITH HOPE

You are my hiding place and my shield; I hope in Your word.

Psalm 119:114, NKJV

Sometimes when life gets tough, we just need someone to have our back. When we have those moments when we feel like we can't keep going or that life is just too hard, it's important to remember what today's Bible verse says.

This verse tells us first that God is our refuge and shield. That means when things get tough, we can go to Him, and He will keep us safe and be a place of refuge. When life gets hard and we have difficulty trying to keep going, we can remember that we can always go to God, and He will be our place to get recharged and feel better about life.

No matter how crazy life gets, we can find hope in God's Word! We also see in this verse that God's Word can be our source of hope. No matter how crazy life gets, we can always have hope. We see in the Bible that we can make it through. God's Word is so important because it gives us hope. We see in it that we can do all things through Christ and that God will never leave us nor forsake us. So even though life sometimes is hard, we can be encouraged to know that God will always take care of us!

The psalmist reminds us of God's wonderful promises and sensible directives for life. His firm conviction is that the Word of God is our best refuge in tough times. Where can we go to remain secure from the onslaught of bad ideas, evil influences, and false hopes? We can go to God and His Word. While people can be disloyal and misguided, God's love is proven through history and through Jesus, and His truth stands forever!!!

Father, thank You for this day and the anchor of hope we have in Jesus. Lord, let Your abundant blessings be our family's portion today. Lord, thank You that Your Word is sure and Your promises to all Your children are unfailing. Lord, thank You that You are our hiding place. Lord, help us to abide in You day by day. Lord, thank You that You are our shield and defender. Lord, please give us Your wisdom as we seek Your will in Your Word. Lord, use us to share the good news of Your life-changing gospel to all those whom we meet today.

Father, we love You. Amen.

NOTES

DO NOT GROW WEARY

And let us not grow weary while doing good, for in due season we shall reap if we do not lose heart.

Galatians 6:9, NKJV

Have you ever started something new, full of excitement, energy, and purpose, only to lose steam halfway through? Sometimes we don't even realize it's happening, but we start drifting from our goals and plans. Maybe the plans changed or the work was harder than we imagined. Maybe unforeseen obstacles presented themselves.

Paul knew that many of the believers in the early church experienced this spiritually. They experienced the genuine conviction of the Spirit, trusted Christ for salvation, and sought to live a life of obedience. But then they experienced persecution. Divisions arose where there was once unity. Their old ways started to pop up again. Paul's encouragement to believers all those generations ago is still applicable to us: don't give up! Keep walking. Keeping moving forward in Jesus' footsteps. Keep seeking to be obedient in everything you do because it isn't in vain.

We might be tempted, after we have walked with Jesus for a while, to believe that it might be in vain. Our service, our worship, our giving, our fellowship, does any of it really have significance in the kingdom? Will we ever see the reward? The fruit of our labor? Because we don't always get to reap the harvest, we might be tempted to stop sowing seeds in the ground.

But Paul reminded us that, though we may not see the reaping, we can continue to drop the seeds and cultivate the soil. Ultimately, we aren't responsible for the harvest. Only God does the harvesting. We are but laborers in His field. Though we might not always see the results, we can trust and not lose heart in the midst of the work!

May the Lord encourage us. May He sustain the work of our hands that we can see the result of our effort in Christ. If we remain faithful to the task that God has assigned to our hands, the question is not *if* we shall reap, but *when* we shall reap. In God's time the reaping will come. The Word of God will *never* fail!!!

Father, thank You for this day and for the Holy Spirit who leads, guides, and directs our way. Lord, open the windows of heaven and shine down Your abundant blessings upon us and our family today. Lord, help us to continue to do the little things that we should do even when we are frustrated at the lack of results. Lord, help us to see that these instructions are building our character for use in Your kingdom. Lord, we praise You for Your mighty power, wisdom, and providence. Lord, sometimes we grow weary; be our strength today. Lord, use us as the example of You to all who cross our path today.

Father, we love You. Amen.

NOTES ______________________________

____

SECURED

All the ends of the world shall remember and turn unto the Lord: and all the kindreds of the nations shall worship before thee. For the kingdom is the Lord's: and He is the governor among the nations.

Psalm 22:27–28, KJV

Strong's Concordance defines "governor" as one who rules or reigns; one to whom is given power and authority. The Bible makes this abundantly clear. So how does this affect us? In what ways can we find comfort in the fact that God is the governor of nations?

For me, it brings peace when I think of all the turmoil in our world. Wars and rumors of wars—yes, we're living in the last days. Peace on earth seems like wishful thinking. But no matter how chaotic things may appear, we can trust that God is in charge, and one day, everyone will answer to Him. He has the final say. He always has and always will reign supreme.

I want to focus on a statement I read that blew me away. Are you ready? It went something like this: "God may have all rule and authority, which doesn't mean He's in total control. Remember, He gave man a free will." What? Really!! God gave man a choice, but that is not to say that He surrendered control to mankind. I know that we live in a wicked world, and sometimes it does seem like things are spinning out of control.

There are days when it feels like God has taken His hands off the situation and said, "Okay, I've given you control. Do the best you can with it." But the fact is that God is always in control. He knows what's going on and even though we don't understand it, the events of today are part of His plan. He is not sitting up in heaven, biting His fingernails and muttering, "Oh, my poor children. I wish I could help them, but it's just not my place since I've given them free will." That's ridiculous!

To me, the saddest part is that I don't know how anyone who believes this nonsense could have any peace in their lives. How could they sleep at night? How could they face life's trials and valleys if they felt that God doesn't have total control of what's happening? I can't imagine such a life, and I'm glad I don't have to. The Bible makes it clear that God is in complete control of *everything*! And with that knowledge, we can rest secure and live in peace. God has it all under control!!!

Father, thank You for this day and the freedom we have in Christ. Lord, let Your abundant blessings flow from heaven over us and our family today. Father, Son, and Holy Spirit, Yours is the kingdom. You rule over us, and indeed over all the nations. Lord, You sit enthroned upon our praises this morning. Lord, help us by the ministry of Your Holy Spirit to walk in victory through this day. Lord, use us to proclaim that You are in full control of everything to all who will listen.

Father, we love You. Amen.

NOTES

DIFFERENCE MAKERS

Wash and make yourselves clean. Take your evil deeds out of my sight; stop doing wrong. Learn to do right; seek justice. Defend the oppressed. Take up the cause of the fatherless; plead the case of the widow.

Isaiah 1:16–17, NIV

It's easy to say that you're a believer in Christ. The hard part is the follow-up that is expected when you make that proclamation to the world! How do we continue to be ourselves, the person whom everyone has known, and begin our journey in Christ effectively and sincerely?

Most of us try the extremes. We separate from the church, or we separate from our friends. Neither one of these actions is good or a benefit to our spiritual maturity. When you say that you're a Christian, but stay away from the church, you risk being tempted beyond your ability to fight, you have the very real potential of not being in your Bible regularly, and you're not connected with God's people to be held accountable to stay on the straight and narrow, among other things.

When we claim to be Christian, but we separate from our friends, we alienate a body of people God wants to us impact. We can be seen as arrogant, which pushes people away, and most importantly, we don't get to see the tangible benefits of our continued change in the presence of our friends, which if we're doing God's business right, will convict them.

So what is there left to do? Well, today's passage speaks volumes to the heart and mindset that we should take up in general. Isolation isn't the answer; rather, cleansing yourself is. We see nine commands in these verses: wash, cleanse, remove, stop, learn, pursue, correct, defend, and plead. These commands will help us get back in step to a worship that is pleasing to the Lord. Let's stop doing it our way, look at His Word, look to where our help comes (not out at our circumstances), and listen to what the Holy Spirit reveals as we read Scripture!

No matter where we are, who we're around, what we used to do, or what people knew us for, when we take up the calling of being in God's kingdom, His family, there should be some things in our life that look different but are easily identifiable. By initiating these very important aspects in our life, we are not only faithfully moving from a life of sin into an existence that glorifies God but also promoting how the effects of God's commands produce the true living reality of a child of God.

Today, let's be clean. Let's put away the evil in our lives and learn to do well. Let's be compassionate and help other people who need justice, mercy, support, guidance, and love. Let's make time to invest in someone with our experiences and help them make better choices. Let's be the people who make the difference for good!!!

Father, thank You for this day and the breath of Your Word that sustains our walk in it. Lord, open the floodgates of heaven and rain down Your abundant blessings upon us and our family today. Lord of all comfort, open our eyes today to see those who need Your love and give us the attentiveness, time, and compassion to serve them. Lord, thank You for this wonderfully forthright Word and for the good news that we are not left in a doleful, miserable condition. Lord, use us to be the hand of Your love to those who need it today.

Father, we love You. Amen.

NOTES

GENEROSITY

The generous soul will be made rich, and he who waters will also be watered himself.

Proverbs 11:25, NKJV

One of the greatest traits any of us can be known for is generosity. For believers in Jesus, our generosity should be patterned after God's. When we stop and think about just how generous God has been to us, it will truly amaze us. Romans 8:32 gives us a great understanding of God's generosity to us. It reads, "He who did not spare his own Son, but gave him up for us all—how will he not also, along with him, graciously give us all things?" (NIV).

So why is it that we often struggle with being generous to others? Is it related to our fear of not having enough? The logic of withholding from others goes like this: *I am afraid I do not have enough, so I cannot afford to be as generous as I would like to be.* God's Word challenges us in this faulty logic. In fact, in Proverbs 11:25 we learn that when we are generous, God will see to it that we will have enough to begin being generous. The real question is simply this: When will we choose to be generous with others with what we have?

If we take God at His Word, the sooner we start, the better. Yes, generosity is the ultimate win-win. Not only will others be refreshed in receiving a gift motivated by love, but we will also be refreshed in the joy of giving and being used by God in this way. So whom is God leading you to be generous toward today? One way to determine this is to ask God to bring someone to mind who needs to be refreshed. When we sense a need along these lines, it will bring us great satisfaction to stop withholding, and to start being generous.

Being generous doesn't have to take a lot of money; it's just about getting out of ourselves and the pursuit of stuff and into being a blessing to other people around us. So today, ask God for ways that you can be generous. Let me caution you, however, that becoming generous can become a contagious activity for all who give it a try.

As we are generous like God, we trust that He will in turn make sure we are blessed and refreshed in the ways that will draw us more and more into His character and more able to help others in the future!!!

Father, thank You for this day and for waking us up and setting us on our journey today. Lord, let Your abundant blessings be our family's portion today. Lord, we thank You for all the great examples of generosity that have graced our lives. Lord, whether rich or poor, these conduits of Your grace have taught us that we too, can be more like You in this way. Lord, bless us with trust and faith as we seek to be more generous with others with our grace, forgiveness, finances, encouragement, and time.

Father, we love You. Amen.

NOTES

HEAVENLY WISDOM

Who is wise and understanding among you? Let them show it by their good life, by deeds done in the humility that comes from wisdom. But if you harbor bitter envy and selfish ambition in your hearts, do not boast about it or deny the truth.

James 3:13–14, NIV

There is a significant difference between true wisdom and false wisdom, between wisdom from above and the wisdom of the world. The world too often equates wisdom with knowledge while godly wisdom comes from above as the Spirit of God directs the steps of our feet and guides us in His actions and attitude.

Wisdom does not depend on how much knowledge we manage to acquire, but on how we conduct ourselves in everyday life. Godly wisdom is exhibited in the way that we apply all that we have learned from the Word of God in our everyday life, and in the decisions and choices we make. When James asked this rhetorical question, he was not expecting any answer, but giving emphasis to the radical differences between wisdom that is given from above and the sort of wisdom that has its roots in all that is earthly, fleshly, worldly, and false.

Envy and strife, together with boasting and deceit, are some of the hallmarks of worldly wisdom. However, the fruit of the Spirit is evidenced in the wisdom that comes from above, where purity and peace join together in perfect union and where meekness and mercy embrace one another. Graciousness and goodness join together with sincerity and truth, which are recognizable garments, and the garments of sincerity and truth, righteousness and grace are only worn by the one who is the benefactor of Christlike wisdom from above.

May this important question be asked of all who are saved by grace through faith in Christ. In God's grace we reflect the beauty and wisdom of the Lord Jesus, both by our good behavior and through the gentleness of spirit, which alone comes from the Lord Himself. So let us remember today, godly wisdom is not about flaunting knowledge but about living a godly life!!!

Father, thank You for this day and thank You that in Christ we have a living example of what a life that is walking in spirit and truth should be. Lord, let Your abundant blessings flow over us and our family today. Lord, may we die to self and live to Christ, so we may say the life that we now live in the flesh is not us but Christ living in us. Lord, please protect us from arrogance and feelings of superiority, and gently humble us in the ways that make us a more useful tool in Your hands. Lord, use us to share the care that You have lavished on us with the people who most need it today.

Father, we love You. Amen.

NOTES ______________________________

____

____

____

HEAVEN'S HARVEST

But the wisdom that comes from heaven is first of all pure; then peace-loving, considerate, submissive, full of mercy and good fruit, impartial and sincere. Peacemakers who sow in peace reap a harvest of righteousness.

James 3:17–18, NIV

Concerning the things that are considered to be smart or the right things to do, James reminds us that the wisdom from above is not at all like the wisdom of this world. God has told us that His ways are higher than our ways, as the heavens are higher than the earth. His thoughts are not like our thoughts, and we don't need to look too far at all in this world to understand that.

Godly wisdom sets itself apart from this world in that first of all it shows itself as pure in an impure world. It does not tolerate others; rather, it is full in an abundance and overflowing with mercy and good deeds. Not good deeds to those who can do us a favor later, but not considering those kinds of human angles or kickbacks. Good deeds done to one and all in Jesus' name, with, as best as we can, no ulterior motivations.

This kind of living and loving represents heaven's harvest. When we plant these kinds of seeds in the grace of Jesus Christ our Lord, we will indeed reap a harvest. What will that be? One that endeavors to be a bridge builder, a peace speaker, and a peacemaker to see people come into a place of right standing with God. God's wisdom reflects who He is, while earthly wisdom reflects the darkness and sin that lie within people's hearts. In order to attain God's wisdom, believers need to ask in faith and humbly receive transformation through God's Word by the power of the Holy Spirit.

True wisdom does not come from a high IQ or from high scores on college entrance exams. True wisdom is a gift from God, given to help us live as God expects us. It is the kind of wisdom that affects every area of our everyday lives. "The wisdom that comes from heaven is first of all pure; then peace-loving, considerate, submissive, full of mercy and good fruit, impartial and sincere." This is the wisdom each one of us needs.

Ask God today and every day to fill you with His wisdom. Pray for the presence of the Holy Spirit to help you experience the wisdom that comes from heaven!!!

Father, thank You for this day and the breath of life. Lord, open the storehouses of Your abundant blessings upon us and our family today. Lord, give us wisdom from above; we cannot produce it on our own. Lord, help us be "peace-loving, considerate, submissive, full of mercy and good fruit, impartial and sincere." Lord, help us see the supreme value of unity and togetherness. Lord, use us to live in the peaceful fruit of righteousness and help others who come our way experience it too.

Father, we love You. Amen.

NOTES ______________________________

WORDS FULL OF SPIRIT AND LIFE

It is the Spirit who gives life; the flesh profits nothing. The words that I speak to you are spirit, and they are life.

John 6:63, NKJV

Do we want others to experience the abundant life that Jesus came to earth, died, and was resurrected for so they might have it? This verse says the Spirit alone gives life. So my question is this: Is it our nature or God's nature flowing through us that is touching the people around us and the people who we hope will experience this abundant and eternal life?

Only when we relinquish our self-nature, when we yield our own self, and allow God's Holy Spirit to flow through our spirits into our souls and outwardly through our bodies will people experience God's Spirit and the life that Jesus wants them to have. Let's be reminded that it is important for us to start out our day asking God to help us surrender ourselves to His will and His Spirit, so He can live through what we do and what we say. This will show that our living comes from His Spirit directly and by His power.

As well, the more frequently we can have this attitude and lift up a similar prayer throughout the day, the more likely it is that our actions and speech will be influenced by God's Holy Spirit and not be of our own soul-nature. This will then increase the likelihood that people we speak to and what we write about will be of God and His Spirit and will have His life in it. This requires intentionality. It requires a choice to live like this. It requires a certain sensitivity, appreciation, and an awareness of when we are living from our soul-nature versus living by the anointing of the Holy Spirit. And then, it requires a degree of obedience to live out God's will instead of our own nature.

We can be sure, then, that if we are acting out of the promptings and from the direction of the Holy Spirit who lives in us, we will be extending true life to others whom we interact with and serve. Only in that way can we be assured that we are being instruments, in the purest sense, of God and His love. Are we being intentional and surrendering our own nature and asking God that His nature and His Holy Spirit guide and live through us? Is it the Spirit who gives life?

The Spirit draws us to Christ, exalts Him as the living Lord, empowers His words, and generates us when we believe. We worship the Father, the Son, and the Holy Spirit. Together, they provide our full salvation. Today, let us warmly receive all that the Spirit does in us!!!

Father, thank You for this day and for waking us up and setting us on our journey through it. Lord, encourage us to look after our spirits and grow in faith. Lord, enable us to accept today as an opportunity to grow closer to You. Lord, we want to honor You as You want to be honored. Lord, we want to hear Your Words and be changed. Lord, we want to receive the Spirit that You have promised and be transformed. Lord, use us to be salt and light to this decaying world.

Father, we love You. Amen.

NOTES

REJOICE ALWAYS

Rejoice always. Pray without ceasing, in everything give thanks; for this is the will of God in Christ Jesus for you.

1 Thessalonians 5:16–18, NKJV

People often say that they really want to know God's will for their lives. Here are three verses that plainly state what God's will is for us in Christ Jesus: "Rejoice always, pray without ceasing, in everything, give thanks; for this is the will of God in Christ Jesus for you." How do we always rejoice? We're to live moment by moment, one day at a time. We're given enough grace for this day to live for Him. Sometimes we're rushing around with a to-do list as long as our arm, when suddenly we remember that we should be rejoicing and living in His deep joy.

I read once that if you want to know how rich you are, make a list of all the wonderful things you have that don't cost any money. I began to think of the great salvation, love, and mercy that are ours, the comfort of the Holy Spirit, and what a friend we have in Jesus. There's the family God's given us, our children and grandchildren, relationships with friends, and our wonderful Christian brothers and sisters. The list is endless. We have so much to rejoice in.

How do we pray without ceasing? As we go about our day, we can breathe our prayer to God, committing our thoughts to Him as we go. It doesn't even have to be by spoken words. We can pray without ceasing by including the Lord in our thoughts and actions. We can pray with our hands, as we make or do something. Or it could even be a whisper to the Lord: "Please help me." How do we give thanks for everything?

As we go through our day, continuing our living conversation, we can be thanking Him for being with us in our situations, giving us strength to meet our needs and grace to meet our difficulties. We can give thanks in pain and in joy. This is His will for us in Christ Jesus. Is there a constant awareness of our ups and downs? Joy comes from knowing we are never alone.

Prayer is the ongoing conversation we have, spirit to Spirit, child to Abba, human with God. Thanksgiving and joy are the great reminders that we have been blessed, no matter what the outward circumstances imply!!!

Father, thank You for this day and the air we breathe. Lord, let Your abundant blessings be our family's portion today. Lord, please help us to remember to be in a "living conversation" with You and go through this day with thanksgiving in our hearts. Lord, give us a deeper appreciation and a more profound awareness of Your presence today. Lord, may our lives reflect the joy You have given us by saving us by grace, and may our hearts always find their home in You. Lord, use us to love others as You them today.

Father, we love You. Amen.

NOTES ______________________________

____

EVERYTHING IS BEAUTIFUL

He has made everything beautiful in its time. He has also set eternity in the human heart; yet no one can fathom what God has done from beginning to end.

Ecclesiastes 3:11, NIV

Life is full of contrasts. We go over mountains, and we go through valleys. We celebrate over our successes, and we struggle through failures. We have wins and we have losses. In weather, there are four seasons. But in our lives, there are dozens of different seasons. And every season of life includes both good and bad times. Life is a combination of contrasting seasons.

All sunshine and no rain make a desert. If we're following God's will, if we're trying to live our lives according to the way God wants us to live, then we'll eventually see that these experiences can have purpose and value in our lives. We may think that the only time we're in God's will is when we're at church or having a quiet time. We can be in God's will as we're cleaning out a closet. We can be in God's will as we're washing the car. We can be in God's will when we move to a new location or stay right where we are.

There's a time and season for everything. Ray Stevens sang a song called "Everything Is Beautiful" that included the lyric "Everything is beautiful in its own way." That's not exactly true. Everything is not beautiful. Cancer is not beautiful. Child abuse is not beautiful. War is not beautiful. This verse says it differently, "He has made everything beautiful in its time." That's very different from "everything is beautiful in its own way." Because the Bible is saying that God can take even the bad things and, in the proper season, turn them around and use them for good in the way He intends. God has painted time with changes.

The kaleidoscopic movement of innumerable processes will be seen in the end as "beautiful in its time." It may look a mess up close, just as putting our face too near a big painting will distort our view of it. Stepping back puts it in better perspective. One day we will step back, look at the finished canvas of life with the Artist by our side, and see it in all its beauty and completeness!!!

Father, thank You for this day and for enlightening us by Your Word to know the limitless potentials you've deposited within us. Lord, open the storehouses of Your abundant blessings and pour them out over us and our family today. Lord, we are determined to affect the world positively through this divine power at work in our Spirit. Lord, You created us to be an eternal being. This world is not our home. Though it is beautiful, it is full of sin. You have destined us to live in heaven with You forever. Lord, use us to share Your mercy and grace with all we meet today.

Father, we love You. Amen.

NOTES

PATH-DRIVEN

Trust in the Lord with all your heart, and lean not on your own understanding; in all your ways acknowledge Him, and He shall direct your paths.

Proverbs 3:5–6, NKJV

At the beginning of each new year, it is common for many people to make resolutions. This passage can be broken up into three resolutions with a single result. First, "trust in the Lord with all your heart." Trust Him, not your family, your bank account, your job, or any other thing. Trust God with all that we are, and all that we have.

Yes, trust can be hard. It involves turning everything over to Him. But it is what we are called to do. Second, "lean not on your own understanding." This may be the hardest thing for us. While we acknowledge that our understanding is flawed, whether of the Bible, God, humanity, creation, etc., we still have a tendency to make it a foundation stone. We "lean" on it for support. It impacts all we do. Instead, we need to lean on the truth of God's Word and the guidance of His Spirit, and lastly, "in all your ways acknowledge Him." How might we go about submitting to the Lord?

A good start is to obey the instructions in His Word. Know the Bible and do what it says. Submission is hard, especially in a culture that values individuality. But it is essential in being a faithful Christ-follower. And if we will do those three things, we can count on Him to "make our paths straight." He will direct us and help us to be successful. Not measured as human success, but success in His kingdom.

Let's trust in the Lord, not depend on our own understanding of things, and submit to Him in everything. Together these three things will make up a winning formula for us!!!

Father, thank You for this last day of the year and the strength to walk in it. Lord, open the windows of heaven and shine down Your abundant blessings upon us and our family today. Lord, every good thing we have in our lives has come because of You. The families we have been blessed with, the protection we have received, the values that we hold, the successes we have enjoyed, the hope we have, the salvation we have received, and the future we anticipate are all ours because of Your grace and not our goodness. Lord, please bless us with wisdom and insight as we seek to live for You in today's confusing and immoral world. Lord, use us to be a witness of Your saving grace to those in need of it today.

Father, we love You. Amen.

NOTES

KNOWN PLANS

"For I know the plans I have for you," declares the L*ORD*, *"plans to prosper you and not to harm you, plans to give you hope and a future. Then you will call on me and come and pray to me, and I will listen to you. You will seek me and find me when you seek me with all your heart."*

Jeremiah 29:11–13, NIV

I confess I worry about our future as a nation. Not because of the flawed leaders in power, but because of how the people are responding in a time when we need unity. I wonder how the Israelites truly felt being exiled in Babylon. Their focus must have been on deliverance, on simply getting past their current, horrible state of expulsion.

I imagine they attacked each other with words as they wrestled with their discomfort and fear. Sound familiar? Then along came Jeremiah to share hope with God's people. "God has a plan, and it's for your good," he told them. Yet before he proclaims their future security, he says this: "Work for the peace and prosperity of the city where I sent you into exile. Pray to the Lord for it, for its welfare will determine your welfare."

Maybe you woke up after the election feeling like a stranger in a strange land. We've not been exiled, but perhaps the state of the country we love leaves us feeling as though we've been banished to an uncomfortable place. The words of the prophet Jeremiah are as relevant for us today as they were for the Israelites in Babylon many years ago. Work for peace and pray. Because the welfare of this nation will determine our own. God does have a plan to give us and our families hope and a bright future.

But how we respond in the midst of the mess will determine whether or not we get to walk into it. When we seek God with our whole heart, with our thoughts and words and action, we will find Him, and He will reveal everything we need to thrive in the chaos. Let us remember with man it is impossible, but with God all things are possible!!!

Father, thank You for this day and the breath of life that is found in Your Word. Lord, let Your abundant blessings pour out over us and our family today. Lord, thank You for securing our future and our hope. We leave every fear and concern with You today. The Lord shows us how to thrive even when life gets messy. Lord, turn our eyes and our ears away from the chatter of the world and toward You. Lord, hear our prayers as we seek peace and unity for our nation, as we follow You with our whole heart. Lead us in how to effectively share Your truth with the world. Lord, use us to be a light that leads others to You out of the darkness of this world.

Father, we love You. Amen.

NOTES ____

IMMOVABLE FOUNDATION

Let the morning bring me word of your unfailing love, for I have put my trust in you. Show me the way I should go, for to you I entrust my life. Rescue me from my enemies, LORD, for I hide myself in you. Teach me to do your will, for you are my God; may your good Spirit lead me on level ground.

Psalm 143:8–10, NIV

This is how we should trust in God as our only refuge and our only hope. This should be our daily prayer: "Teach me to do Your will, for You are my God." Our hearts should long for the lovingkindness of God. To hear Him speak in words of steadfast love. Each day without delay our hearts should call out to God.

To seek His guidance in the way we should walk, that our lives would bring Him honor and glory. God's divine guidance is surely indispensable, for only a Christ-driven life is effective, enjoyable, and pleasing to God. In Christ we have peace and security. Under His wings we can find comfort and refuge from the threat of our enemies. Christ is our rescuer and protector. Only in the Lord should we trust.

Therefore, it should be our deepest desire to know the will of God, and to have a heart to obey God's will, for He is our God and Lord over our lives. In our life journey here on earth, there will be good times and bad, but through it all, with God as our guide, we will make it through the trials and tribulations.

But how can God teach us His ways so that we walk in His ways? Well, God has laid out His plan and purposes for us in His Word, and the Bible should be the immovable foundation upon which our trust in God is founded. He clearly lays out the path that we are to follow, and we should read, mark, learn, and inwardly digest the Word of God with an undivided heart, so that in the power of the Holy Spirit we may grow in grace and in knowledge of the Lord Jesus, for this is the will of God in each of our lives: that we should know God and Jesus Christ whom He has sent. God bless, and have a great day in God's Word!!!

Father, thank You for this day and Your amazing grace. Lord, open the floodgates of heaven and rain down Your abundant blessings upon us and our family today. Lord, we commit ourselves to You and to Your Word each day. Lord, we trust You to lead us through every difficult situation we face. Lord, we ask for Your guidance and direction every step of the way, and we promise to do our best to give ourselves wholeheartedly to Your ways. Lord, use us to be the light of Your love to all whom we meet today.

Father, we love You. Amen.

NOTES

BE STILL

Be still, and know that I am God; I will be exalted among the nations. I will be exalted in the earth!

Psalm 46:10, NKJV

We frequently read this verse as God's command for us to cease from our busy schedules and make time for prayer or worship. Though this is obviously incredibly important, there is a deeper meaning to this verse. When we read the context in which this verse is situated, we may be surprised to discover that when God utters the command, "Be still, and know that I am God," He is not speaking to His people, but to the raging and violent nations who threaten them.

The psalmist is proclaiming that amidst the chaos and turmoil of this world, he rests in the knowledge that God is his refuge. He imagines God as a mighty warrior, fighting against the nations and kingdoms of this world, and even against the mountains and the sea, calling them to be still and recognize Him as God, all for the sake of giving His people a place of refuge, a city that cannot be moved.

We too have many forces arrayed against us, finances, unforeseen calamities, interpersonal conflicts, debilitating illnesses, uncertain futures, and spiritual oppression, and we may feel as though we are tossed about by tides and waves over which we have no control. However, in these moments of trial, when the waters roar and foam, and the mountains tremble with its tumult, we can trust that the Lord Almighty is with us and He makes all troubles still. In the present, nations roar and kingdoms totter, but we look to the future in which God will truly and finally make all wars cease, when He will break the bow, shatter the spear, and burn the shields with fire.

Like Jesus rebuking the storm at sea, God will shout, "Be still!" to all the chaos of this world. So even though in this particular verse, the command to "be still" is not addressed directly to us, it certainly still applies to us. For when we are confident that God has the power to still all that with which the world can threaten us, we too can be still and abide in our knowledge that He, the Lord Almighty, is our refuge!!!

Father, thank You for this day and for waking us up and setting us on our journey through it. Lord, let Your abundant blessings be our family's portion today. Lord, we praise You that Your Word stands fast forever and ever and that Your precious promises encourage us to rest in Your love and drink deeply from the rock of our salvation. Lord, we pray for the salvation of the lost and for Your return, when Your name be exalted throughout all the earth and the nations will know that You are God. Lord, use us to share the gospel of grace to those who cross our path today.

Father, we love You. Amen.

NOTES

CALLED BY NAME

If My people who are called by My name will humble themselves, and pray and seek My face, and turn from their wicked ways, then I will hear from heaven, and will forgive their sin and will heal their land.

2 Chronicles 7:14, NKJV

We want God to heal our land, and we want our nation to change. But as we look at the problems in our country, we want to point at someone else a lot of times. We say the problems are due to Washington, DC, Hollywood, or the White House, but God says the source of the problems is His house, the church. God lays out His prescription in 2 Chronicles 7:14: "If My people who are called by My name will humble themselves, and pray and seek My face, and turn from their wicked ways, then I will hear from heaven, and will forgive their sin and will heal their land."

Notice God says, "If My people who are called by My name." He doesn't say a thing about secular culture. He talks to His own people. That is you. That is me. "If My people." One of the problems in our nation today is there are a lot of people who think they are Christians, but they really are not. In fact, the Bible says, "Examine yourselves as to whether you are in the faith. Test yourselves. Do you not know yourselves, that Jesus Christ is in you?—unless indeed you are disqualified" (2 Cor. 13:5, NKJV).

Then there are those who are living a double life. They put on a good performance at church. They say all the right things. But they are living a life that is completely contradictory to what the Bible says about how a Christian ought to live. A spiritual awakening starts with God's people. It starts with you and me. If we want our churches and our country to see revival, today is the day to seek the Holy Spirit. If we want our communities to see a mighty outpouring of His power, today is the day to seek Jesus.

If God is tugging at our heart today, we need to humble ourselves, pray, seek God's face, turn from our wicked ways, and then we will hear from heaven and God will forgive our sins and heal our lives, families, churches, communities, and our country. And then there can be once more a great revival. Revival does not come from the White House but from God's people in the church house. We are the people of God. We are Christians, known by the name of Jesus.

We need to pray and ask God to come down and pour His Spirit out to turn the hearts of people toward Himself, to open their blind eyes, to set the captives free. We as the people of God need to humble ourselves, repent, and seek God!!!

Father, thank You for this day and for Your Word and the truth that it contains. Lord, open the storehouses of Your abundant blessings and let them flow over us and our family today. Lord, how we praise You for the faithfulness that You show to Your people and for the goodness and grace You have bestowed on the church. Lord, thank You for the many lessons that we learn from Your Word: Your goodness and grace, Your righteous character, and Your merciful nature and faithfulness. Lord, keep us faithful in prayer for those in authority, for kings and presidents, for nations, and for Your people. Lord, we come humbly asking that you reassert Yourself in our nation at this time in clearly recognizable ways. Lord, use us to be salt and light in this dark world.

Father, we love You. Amen.

NOTES

FRUIT BEARER

I am the vine, you are the branches. He who abides in Me and I in him, bears much fruit; for without Me you can do nothing.

John 15: 5, NKJV

The image of a branch gaining all its sustenance and strength from the vine is a beautiful description of our total dependence upon God, without whom we can do nothing, for in Him we live and move and have our being. When Jesus walked the earth, He demonstrated this truth, for He lived His entire life in utter dependence upon the Father. "I can do nothing of Myself," He said. "I speak only that which I have seen from My Father." Though Jesus Christ was fully God, He lived His life in His humanity.

Jesus lived as God intended man to live, in utter dependence upon God. Christ walked in Spirit and truth and only said and did those things that He heard from the Father. He demonstrated how we should live. He lived His life so the life of God could be lived through Him in His humanity. Although Jesus Christ was fully God, He drew all His strength from His Father in heaven, demonstrating how you and I should live as God's children, drawing all our strength from Jesus—for without Him we can do nothing.

We are to walk in Spirit and truth and to do only those things that we hear from Christ our Savior, so that His life may be lived in us and through us. Until we humbly confess that in and of ourselves, we can do nothing. We will foolishly and unsuccessfully attempt to produce good fruit in our own strength.

Let us meditate on the vital principle that Jesus is the vine and we are the branches. We are to abide in Him and allow His Spirit to live through us, just as He abode in the Father and did only those things that He heard from the Father. For apart from Him, we can do nothing!!!

Father, thank You for this day and sustenance we get from abiding in Jesus. Lord, pour out Your abundant blessings over us and our family today. Lord, teach us to live as You would have us to live in total dependence upon You. Lord, increase our desire to seek You, know You, and remain close to You. Lord, help us to be faithful and not give up when we are tired and weary. Lord, help us to endure Your pruning with grace and strength. Lord, help us to stay fully connected to You, the true vine, and receive all that You are and all that You desire for us. Lord, fashion Your character in us and use us today to bless others.

Father, we love You. Amen.

NOTES ________________________________

____

____

____

RISE AND STAND UPRIGHT

Some trust in chariots and some in horses, but we trust in the name of the LORD our God. They are brought to their knees and fall, but we rise up and stand firm.

Psalm 20:7–8, NKJV

For people in the modern world, trusting in chariots and horses may seem like a pleasant metaphor, but remember, these were prime examples of human power and might in the ancient world.

Therefore, I wonder how David would have written this verse in 2020. "Some trust in science." "Some trust in politicians." "Some trust in the economy." And what are we trusting to get us through this chaos in our nation and this global pandemic? Well, in one sense, we are trusting in human power. If we're sick, we trust in a doctor to provide care. If our business is struggling to make ends meet, we trust in a bank to provide loans. If we lose our jobs, we trust in the government for unemployment. And we trusted in doctors, scientists, and epidemiologists to create a vaccine for diseases.

Now there's nothing inherently wrong with this kind of trust. I'm sure that David placed a certain kind of trust in his horses and mighty men of war. But he knew not to place his ultimate trust in human might and wisdom. That's why he says that those who trust in chariots and horses will "collapse and fall." But those who trust in the name of the Lord will "rise and stand upright." In other words, placing our ultimate trust in human beings doesn't work. On the other hand, placing our ultimate hope in the Lord always works out.

So in this current state of our nation, we can place limited trust in doctors, bankers, politicians, and epidemiologists. But thankfully, our ultimate trust is in the Lord God Almighty who will never fail. This is why we don't put our trust in anything in this world because our God is greater than everything in this world. Our God is the only one who is truly reliable and ultimately the only place we can be assured our trust is safe.

Our God is the only one who is worthy of all of our trust, all of our hopes, and all of our plans. All of our dreams can be trusted with God. All of our lives, our families, our work, indeed everything that we are, we can trust with God. His name is worthy of our trust!!!

Father, thank You for this day and for Your amazing grace. Lord, open the floodgates of heaven and pour out Your abundant blessings over us and our family today. Lord, we pray that we deliberately turn aside from trusting anyone or anything in this world but You. Lord, You ultimately are where we place our trust, and as long as our trust is in You, we can never be moved because You are all powerful, You are all wise, You are all good, You are all loving, and You are totally worthy of all of our trust. Lord, help us to trust You fully, completely, and wholeheartedly today, even with things in our lives right now that we don't understand why this or that is happening. Lord, use us to be the lamp of Your love to all today.

Father, we love You. Amen.

NOTES

GOD'S POWERFUL PRESENCE

For God has not given us a spirit of fear, but of power and of love and of a sound mind.

2 Timothy 1:7, NKJV

What is it that you fear? I have dealt with some fear in my life. On the surface, I fear tight enclosed places, but down deeper, maybe the fear is loss of control. I think many of us fear failure, rejection, or even pain. At times I think we even fear speaking from the depth of our hearts, because we want to be accepted and loved.

Fear speaking from the depth of our hearts because we want to be accepted and loved. Fear can trap us. It takes away our power, and the Lord said that He didn't give us fear but power! Fear, as an emotion, will come at us from time to time and try to stop us dead in our tracks. Fear will keep us tethered like a ball to a pole. It can only go in circles. It can't really fly, and the Lord wants us as believers to soar!

In Paul's statement to Timothy, you might note that he doesn't say that God is referring to those "strong, courageous, powerful, or influential people." He simply refers to "us." The Lord did not give "us" a spirit of fear. He is speaking of you and me. I believe that the Lord wants us to look fear straight in the eye and see it for what it is and for what it isn't. The Spirit of fear is not something that comes from our Creator. It is something the devil uses to stop us in our tracks. It can literally put a roadblock in our life, as you find yourself tethered to it going in circles. The Bible says 365 times to "fear not." I always wonder if that was because God knew that every day we would need a reminder that He is with us, that whatever we fear, He will walk through with us.

When fear of any kind begins to try to invade our mind and our life, it is not the time to succumb to it, it is the time to stand, to remind ourselves that F.E.A.R. is really just False Evidence Appearing Real. Most of the things we fear haven't even happened yet. We are dealing with false evidence. But it can *appear* to be real to us.

Remember, fear is a spirit that doesn't come from God. What is it today that you fear? What holds you back? Today, bring it before His throne and ask Him to give you healing strength in spite of yourself. And remember that our God created us to soar. The indwelling presence of the Holy Spirit brings us power, love, and self-discipline. We shouldn't be timid. The powerful presence of our almighty God lives within us!!!

Father, thank You for this day and breath of Your Word. Lord, let Your abundant blessings flow over us and our family today. Lord, we praise and thank You for Your indwelling Holy Spirit and thank You that our life is hid with Christ in God. Lord, thank You that You have not given us a Spirit of fearfulness, but one of power and love and of a sound mind. Lord, may we not fear rejection or ridicule in this increasingly hostile world. Lord, please fill us with your Spirit, so that we can be a person of character and compassion, demonstrating power, love, and self-discipline in our lives. Lord, use us to be a bold witness of Your mercy and grace to others today.

Father, we love You. Amen.

NOTES

BE ON GUARD

Be on your guard; stand firm in the faith; be courageous; be strong. Do everything in love.

1 Corinthians 16:13–14, NIV

Here are a few things that Paul says to the church of Corinth, which seems to be a timely word for our day. 1) Be on your guard! We never know where temptation and sin will come from, nor when they will hit us. However, we can learn from our failures and mistakes. We can figure out that being tired makes us vulnerable to impatience. We can be alert to what we know. We don't need to be surprised by everything. 2) Stand firm in the faith! Many people attack our faith in many ways. We must stand firm in believing in the creation, the great flood, and the other miracles of the Bible. We must retain confidence in the God who cannot lie. We must believe in the accuracy of the Bible. We must trust in Jesus Christ, even when others waver. 3) Act like men!

Our world needs men who are willing to walk courageously. We need women who are willing to be brave. We must take initiative to protect and provide for others. We must approach life with courage and a sense of responsibility. 4) Be strong! Our strength comes from reliance upon God. We become strong by reading and thinking deeply about the message from God. We become strong by praying and by noticing God's answers to our prayers. We become strong from the support and encouragement of other believers. With strength, we can approach life with confidence. In addition, we are prepared to carry out the next command: 5) Let all that you do be done in love. We can find ways to live in a way that benefits everyone.

We can be kind and patient. We can make the sacrifices. We can honor Jesus Christ through our lives of love. We will never be able to agree on everything with everyone, we're not supposed to, and that's not really the goal. We should never long to look just like the world, out of the fear that we look too different than those around us. We should not be persuaded to live in shades of gray because we don't want to step on any toes. We're here to be salt. We're here to be light. We're here to make a difference, to point others to Christ. And we can be all that God calls us to be, staying strong, staying firm, living aware, walking in love, being people of courage, for this is what matters most anyway!!!

Father, thank You for this day and Your goodness to us and for instructing us on how to live godly lives to Your praise and glory. Lord, open the storehouses of Your abundant blessings over us and our family today. Lord, may we stand firm in the faith and act in a way that does not dishonor Your name. Lord, may we be alert to the evils that surround us and our brothers and sisters in Christ, and may we never compromise the truth of the glorious gospel of grace, but be strong in the Lord and in the power of His might. Lord, help us to withstand the wiles of the devil and be alert to his evil ways. Lord, use us to be a light that leads others from the darkness of this world to You.

Father, we love You. Amen.

NOTES

GREAT COMMANDMENTS

Jesus said to him, "You shall love the LORD your God with all your heart, with all your soul, and with all your mind." This is the first and great commandment. And the second is like it: "You shall love your neighbor as yourself."

Matthew 22:37–39, NKJV

There are three great relationships in life: our relationship with God; our relationship with self; and our relationship with other people. Our life is like a cross with vertical (Godward) and horizontal (manward) lines interesting at the point of self. If we look at the Ten Commandments, we see that the first four have to do with our relationship to God while the last six have to do with our relationship to others.

Our Lord Jesus taught us the same thing. The first and greatest commandment is to love God, and the second is to love our neighbor. Interestingly, self is given a much less important third place, almost an afterthought; we are to love others as we love ourselves. The biblical emphasis is loving outward. The vertical is always the first and most important relationship. God is our creator and sustainer; therefore, He has the first claim on our lives. God has shown us the greatest love in Jesus, so how we respond to this love is of the utmost importance.

Our relationships with the people around us come and go, but our relationship with God will continue forever. A true

Christian ethic must always start here. The horizontal relationship is firmly in second place. When everything is working right, our love for others should flow out of our love for God. If we do not love people whom we have seen, how will we love God whom we have not seen? We need to love the people around us truly and actively.

Our love should be clearly seen in the things we say and do. In third place is self. Yes, we should love ourselves. At the same time for most people this is not the problem. Whether they think so or not, most people love themselves more than they love others. This is seen in practical examples of seeking our own good and comfort before that of others. Instead, we should seek to love others as much as we love ourselves.

It is not about us; it is about God and others. In a holy heart, self is happily and rightly minimized. In all of these relationships the standard, ethic, and goal is love. Love seeks what is best for others. Let us today love God with our whole self. Love others as ourselves!!!

Father, thank You for this day and loving us when we were dead in our sins and for bringing us into Your family, simply because we trusted the Lord Jesus as Savior. Lord, we want to love You with every part of our being. Lord, may we live as You would choose and love You with all our heart and soul and strength and mind. Lord, please accept the work of our hands, the words of our mouth, the moments of our rest, and the love of our heart as our worship to You this day. Lord, use us to be the depth of Your love to all who need it today.

Father, we love You. Amen.

NOTES

WAIT ON THE LORD

But those who wait on the LORD shall renew their strength; they shall mount up with wings like eagles; they shall run and not be weary; they shall walk and not faint.

Isaiah 40:31, NKJV

If we wait upon the Lord, He will renew our strength. We can spread our wings and soar high as eagles do. Though at times we can feel weary, God strengthens us with His power, and He renews us. We don't have to let our circumstances or the chaos in our country overwhelm us and keep us down, unable to see beyond it. If we look up to God, committing our ways to Him and giving over our cares, we can rise up and soar above all our circumstances. We then will be able to run and not be weary, to walk and not faint (or become tired).

If you are feeling exhausted and weary and in need of an energy boost, give it over to God and continue to give it over moment by moment. Allow Him to strengthen you, so you can soar above it. If we rise up and soar as eagles do, our circumstances won't overwhelm us. When we are weary from the struggles of life and find it hard to keep going, we can turn to God and ask Him for renewal and strength. Our great God gloriously provides power to those who pursue His presence and fully rely on Him.

As we patiently rest in His care with expectation, He brings His healing and hope to help us take flight and finish with fresh enthusiasm and energy. Are you flapping your wings in your own energy right now? Are you weary from struggling to solve your problems with your own strength? Slow down and spend time with God who is more powerful than your problems. Ask Him to fill you with a renewed hope. Trust that He is at work and knows the way. We will always soar when we surrender to God.

It is inevitable that on occasion we will feel the weariness of life weighing us down. When you find yourself in the that place today, ask the Lord to renew your spiritual strength. Whatever stands in your path, God can give you the strength to face it and rise above it!!!

Father, thank You for this day and the breath of life that is in Your Word. Lord, open the floodgates of heaven and rain down Your abundant blessings upon us and our family today. Lord, we know that our strength can only be found in You. Lord, help us to trust implicitly in the power that we can only receive from You. Lord, we pray that we may truly rise above all the difficulties of life and run with patient endurance the race that is set before us, looking unto You, who is our only source of strength and our only means of refreshment. Lord, use us to be the salt and light of Your Word to help others find their way to You.

Father, we love You. Amen.

NOTES

CLOTHED

I delight greatly in the LORD; my soul rejoices in my God. For he has clothed me with garments of salvation and arrayed me in a robe of his righteousness, as a bridegroom adorns his head like a priest, and as a bride adorns herself with her jewels.

Isaiah 61:10, NIV

Take a moment to think about what God has done for you and what He has given you. Remember what you deserve and are not getting. This should cause extreme delight in God's great love and mercy for you. Find your strength in what God has done for you and rejoice in that. Give God praise for the salvation and righteousness He has blessed you with. Nothing could be better than that.

What a cause of great joy and rejoicing to know that the gifts of God are glorious and without number. Who can count the many blessings that are showered down on each one of us day by day? He pours out gifts of the Spirit and gifts for the soul, and all His many gifts and graces to us are yes and amen in Christ. But the greatest gift of all is the garment of His salvation and the clean robe of His own precious righteousness, for greater than the gifts of God is the giver of all who has come to dwell in the hearts of all who believe in His name.

May we cultivate an attitude of humble gratitude and joyful thanksgiving for it is good to sing praises to the God of our salvation, for He has clothed us with the garments of salvation and has covered us with His robe of righteousness. These garments cannot be purchased, nor can they be made by your own hands.

The garments have already been provided, and the Lord has chosen us to wear them. He knows us, yet we are chosen, holy, and beloved. Do you want to be dressed appropriately? Do you want to be dressed in a suitable and fitting way? Ask the Lord, and He will help you!!!

Father, thank You for this day and Your many gifts of pardon, peace, and purity, of faith, hope, and love. Lord, let Your abundant blessings be our portion this day. Lord, above all, we bless and thank You for the greatest of all gifts, which is the person of Yourself, who died to redeem us with His precious blood and who lives forever within our hearts. Lord, thank You for paying the price for our sins to give us life. Holy Spirit, thank You for the revelation that Jesus cleansed us from our sin and empowers us to live for God. Lord, use us to live in such a way that those around us know that You have made us whole and holy and that Your desire is to do it for them.

Father, we love You. Amen.

NOTES ______________________________

____

____

____

IN STEP

Since we live by the Spirit, let us keep in step with the Spirit.

Galatians 5:25, NIV

From the moment we receive Christ, we live in the Spirit. He is always with us, to guide our steps, to bear witness with our spirit, and to let us know that we belong to God. The Spirit enlightens our understanding, and when needed, He confronts and corrects us when we get out of His will. To live by the Spirit involves active obedience to His direction.

When we live in the Spirit and walk in the Spirit and let the Spirit lead us, it will be toward more and more of Christ, for He will kindle in our hearts more love for the Savior, and we will become more deeply interested in the work of our Redeemer. The result will be that we will care less for the world and develop a greater love for Jesus and focus only on what is holy and pure. We need to remember that light drives out darkness, love expels hate, and holiness removes sin.

When we place our faith in Jesus as our Savior, His Spirit comes to live within us. Then He works to transform us, replacing our selfishness with Christlikeness. As we grow in grace and in our knowledge of God, our thoughts, words, and actions become more like our Lord's. To walk means we should be in fellowship with the Holy Spirit.

This means a disciplined walk in the things of God. God is interested in every part of our lives; therefore, we need to submit every aspect of our lives to Him: the emotional, physical, social, intellectual, and vocational. We must walk in the Spirit. This means relying on the Helper to produce spiritual fruit in our lives. To walk in the Spirit means to follow His leadership each moment of the day, permitting His power to be in our life, and the result of this walk will be the fruit of the Spirit that we will produce.

For this reason, let us trust confidently in the Spirit's power and promise to give us that enablement as we obediently live and walk in the Spirit!!!

Father, thank You for this day and the Holy Spirit who is our guide. Lord, open the storehouses of Your abundant blessings and shower them over us and family today. Lord, thank You that at the point of our salvation, we were made alive in the Spirit and became one with You. Lord, we pray that we may live the rest of our lives walking in spirit and truth. Lord, thank You for the gift of Your Spirit who is alive in us. Lord, may Your Spirit guide our thoughts and mold us to be like You in words and deeds. Lord, use us to be a blessing in someone's life today.

Father, we love You. Amen.

NOTES

DO NOT BE AFRAID OR DISCOURAGED

Keep this Book of the Law always on your lips; meditate on it day and night, so that you may be careful to do everything written in it. Then you will be prosperous and successful. Have I not commanded you? Be strong and courageous. Do not be afraid; do not be discouraged, for the Lord *your God will be with you wherever you go.*

Joshua 1:8–9, NIV

Did it ever occur to us that we serve the same God as Joshua? The challenge to be strong and courageous is God's challenge to believer's today. God's presence and protection are available to all believers in Christ. It is still God's desire for every believer to read, obey, meditate, and do what the Bible says.

We are commanded to tell others about our Savior and Lord, Jesus Christ. This is where our battle begins. We must go in the power of the Holy Spirit with strength and courage. American culture is no longer centered on truth. It, instead, revolves around opinion, fake news, shaming, and division. There are at least two sides to every issue, and Christians on both sides tend to be strong and courageous to fuel their desire to widen the chasm between themselves and their perceived enemies.

The result is Christians who should be loving each other and taking care of the world as a unified force are demeaning each other based on their voting choices and touting infighting as courageous. The bottom line of this passage is that despite the repetitions of being strong and courageous, it's not truly about Joshua's strength or courage. It's about Joshua being told, rather, commanded, to seek God first above all else and make sure Israel does the same.

Why? Because Joshua can only be strong and courageous if his strength and courage come from the Lord and not his own power. Joshua is asked to model three behaviors, which all apply directly to us today. 1) Remember God's promises (v. 6); 2) remember God's principles (v. 7–8); 3) and remember God's presence (v. 9). Joshua simply had to trust the promise of the Lord and act upon it. And we too are to know the truth of God's Word and to meditate on the promises of God, to trust in the truth of God's Word, and to follow the instructions that have been laid out in Scripture!!!

Father, thank You for this day, and we praise You that You have shown Yourself faithful to Your people, throughout all generations. Lord, let Your abundant blessings flow over us and our family today. Lord, help us to be strong in You and to rely on You in all the problems of life that we may face, knowing that You are with us wherever we go. Lord, who is and was and is to come, thank You for being there and staying there when all others forsake and leave. Lord, You are the one constant in our lives so full of change. Lord, use us to share the blessing of Your saving grace that someone needs today.

Father, we love You. Amen.

NOTES

PEACEFUL THANKFULNESS

Let the peace of Christ rule in your hearts, since as members of one body you were called to peace. And be thankful. Let the message of Christ dwell among you richly as you teach and admonish one another with all wisdom through psalms, hymns, and songs from the Spirit, singing to God with gratitude in your hearts. And whatever you do, whether in word or deed, do it all in the name of the Lord Jesus, giving thanks to God the Father through him.

Colossians 3:15–17, NIV

Often how we approach God as our heavenly Father, we ask, ask, and ask because we know He cares. Unfortunately, we don't always make the time to praise Him for who He is and thank Him for what He's done. Eventually, this will lead to a me-centered attitude in our relationships with others, our relationship with God, and how we approach every arena of our life.

Our gratitude produces the peace of Christ that passes all understanding that supports our spiritual growth, along with the church's health, hope, and connectedness. We must allow the Word of God to impact us, live in us, and referee us so we can live joyfully, worship God, and love others more effectively.

Christ is the one who has to empower us not only to save us but also so we can trust in Him for holy living.

With the understanding of what Christ did for us, we can have the hope and confidence to trust and obey Him. These are the attributes that produce character and spiritual maturity that in turn show that we are representatives of Christ. This total life transformation will not only change us from the inside out but also allow us to have an impact on others for the kingdom. We need to permit the Holy Spirit to be our guide, the one who reveals sin in our lives that needs to be confessed, the one who opens out hearts and minds to the treasures in Scripture, and the one who gives us the desire and the power to do the will of God.

Remember, we belong to Christ; hence, we bear the name Christian. We are His ambassadors in this time and place. Many times, we are the only Bible people see. So the question today is what will they see when we are in our home, neighborhood, workplace, classroom, at the store, etc. What will they see when we encounter trials and tribulations?

May we with one accord let the peace of Christ rule in our hearts day by day and moment by moment, for it is to this that the body in Christ has been called. And let us in all things be thankful!!!

Father, thank You for this day and the breath of life that is Your Word. Lord, let Your abundant blessings flow from the windows of heaven over us and our family today. Lord, let Your peace rule in our hearts, and let us be at peace in His one body. Lord, fill our hearts and mouths with overflowing thanksgiving. Lord, dwell in us richly, and teach and admonish each of us in all wisdom. Lord, help us to impart grace through the songs flowing from our thankful hearts. Lord, may we honor You in all we say and do, and we pray that we may grow more like You in our dealings with others today. Lord, use us to be the touch of Your love to all today.

Father, we love You. Amen.

NOTES

PRAYERFUL REQUEST

Be anxious for nothing, but in everything by prayer and supplication, with thanksgiving, let your requests be made known to God; and the peace of God, which surpasses all understanding, will guard your hearts and minds through Christ Jesus.

Philippians 4:6–7, NKJV

Prayer is the privilege of people who are saved by grace through faith in Christ. For by His sacrificial death and glorious resurrection, He tore down the dividing wall between God and us, and then gave us access to His throne of grace to find help and mercy in time of need. We are exhorted not to worry about anything, but instead to pray confidently about everything.

When I read these verses this morning, I saw something fresh. Paul is instructing us to stop worrying and go to God with prayer and supplication. Then we are to thank Him for the answer. But Paul says nothing about receiving deliverance, a word of direction, miracles, or healing. Instead, he says that we receive a gift: the peace of God. God answers all our requests and supplication with the gift of His peace.

So how do we shed our anxiousness? Well, God tells us that we should pray to Him with thanksgiving and make our request known to Him. Stressed out? Pray. Worried? Pray. Anxious? Pray. I think at times our problems look so big because we have taken our focus off God and put all the focus on our problems. He is so much bigger than our problems. He's our healer, our provider, our shelter, our everything, so sometimes we need to remember whom we should be focusing on.

All praying people have one thing in common: no matter how bad we may feel going into our secret closet of prayer, we come out filled with His peace. Many of us wrestle with the Lord in prayer. We petition Him with many tears, we pound heaven's gates, and we claim every promise. But as the days, weeks, and months go by, we begin to wonder. *Why won't He hear us? What's blocking our prayer?* The fact is God already has said to us, "Here! Here is My peace, and it passes all understanding. Take it and let it rule in your heart while I work all things for your good!!!"

Father, thank You for this day and that You know all things and that You know everything about us. Lord, let Your abundant blessings flow over us and our family today. Lord, thank You that You hold today in Your hand and our future is secure in You. Lord, thank You that we can cast all our cares upon You, for You care for us. Lord, thank You that You are known for doing what seems impossible. Lord, we bring our requests to You and in faith trust You to meet our every need. Lord, thank You for covering us in Your peace while we wait for Your answers to our prayers and Your direction in our lives. Lord, use us to be the light to those who are lost in the darkness of this world today.

Father, we love You. Amen.

NOTES

SALT AND LIGHT

You are the salt of the earth. But if the salt loses its saltiness, how can it be made salty again? It is no longer good for anything, except to be thrown out and trampled underfoot. You are the light of the world. A town built on a hill cannot be hidden.

Matthew 5:13–14, NIV

Every Christian is called by God to be an influence on the world around them. Jesus began teaching this concept early in His ministry when He told His disciples that He would make them fishers of men. Then He used illustrations of salt and light. Both salt and light have properties that affect things around them. Salt is used to enhance flavor and act as a preservative.

To be salt means to deliberately seek to influence the people in one's life by showing them the unconditional love of Christ through good deeds. Light is a symbol used to mean awareness, knowledge, and understanding. To be a light means to be a witness to others concerning the truth of God's Word, especially about who Christ is and how He died and rose again for our salvation.

As God's redeemed people, we possess the Word of God, and we are salt and light in the world. Gradually, throughout Jesus' teaching ministry, He refined this idea that each one who followed Him was to have a spiritual impact on those around them. He has sent us out to everyone around us to share His mercy and grace and their need of repentance and the coming of the kingdom of God. Let us live our lives unto the Lord and to His praise and glory, so that we may not waste this life of ours but be a worthy witness to the goodness and grace of our heavenly Father. He loved the world so much that He gave His only begotten Son, so that whoever believes in Him would not perish but have everlasting life.

In humility and submission to God, we work for right relations, for merciful actions, and for peace. When we live as people of blessing, we are salt and light—in the workplace, in our homes, and in our nation. So be encouraged today. You are precious, valuable, and you are the preservative that God is using in the earth today! Go and be the salt of the earth!!!

Father, thank You for this day and Your Word of life that sustains us. Lord, open the windows of heaven and pour out Your abundant blessings upon us and our family today. Lord, we pray that we may be a worthy witness and become salt and light in this world to Your glory. Lord, help us to be Your light of joy and salvation that will help others come to know You. Lord, we pray that our words and actions and all that we are will be seasoned with salt and that You would use us to be a witness to Your goodness and grace.

Father, we love You. Amen.

NOTES ______________________________

____

____

TESTIMONY

I was born on June 4, 1964, in Hugo, Oklahoma, and came to Dallas in 1970. I watched my parents struggle raising two boys and fight a lot, which led them to divorce when I was eleven. Beginning at the age of eleven, I started experimenting with drugs and alcohol to escape the pain of what I was experiencing. I also became very promiscuous after being molested at the young age of twelve.

I accepted the Lord as my Savior at the age of thirteen, but quickly denounced Him after being told by a pastor that I was going to hell for not attending church every Sunday. I spent the next sixteen years of my life telling anyone who would listen that I was Satan's child, and my life surely showed it. Eight of those sixteen years I went off the deep end into drugs, alcohol, and promiscuity. I had to be good at hiding it because I was a good athlete who excelled in sports in school.

So no one knew that I was heavily off into the drug scene except those doing the drugs with me. After graduating high school I got married to a woman with a two-year-old daughter, and we divorced that same year. I again went off the deep end drinking, drugging, and living promiscuously. At the age of twenty-two I again married a woman with two daughters. At the age of twenty-two I finally gave up the drugs, alcohol, and promiscuity, but I was still living a life without hope.

I started going to church with my family, and on March 25, 1992, I authentically gave my life over to Jesus. In August of that year we had a daughter, and in 1998 we adopted a nine-year-old daughter. I was in the church every time the door was open but did not know what walking with Jesus even meant.

On December 7, 2005, my little brother was killed in a car wreck, and I struggled with the fact that we were at odds with each other and barely talking. In 2007 God called, and I was ordained as a pastor.

On January 2, 2015, our adopted daughter was killed in a car wreck along with her boyfriend, and I struggled with the fact that I was estranged from her due to her life choices. In 2017 Satan convinced me that life was not worth living after my personal life came undone, so I tried to kill myself, but God intervened and saved me. I heard Him say He was not through with me yet. I can say emphatically He uses the broken life after all the life has been broken to nothing but dust, ensuring that we cannot put the pieces of our life back together ourselves.

After this encounter with God, I realized I was saved but not free. God led me to the cave, just like He did Elijah in 1 Kings 19:1–18, until I was able to hear the whisper of His voice that would lead to an intentional intimacy with Him. I spent 2017–2020 releasing the things that were holding my soul in bondage and forgiving my loved ones, people, and the past. I discovered that I knew who God was, but not who He is or who I was in Him.

So I started the journey and I have not completely arrived, but I am engaging in intentional intimacy with God through prayer, studying the Scriptures, and sharing my faith. I was a boy who let the world shape his early manhood, lost without hope to a man seeking hope in Christ, realizing he was existing in the busyness of relationship with Christ instead of sitting in an intentional intimate relationship with Him.

I am a man who has discovered his insatiable desire to be in the audience of one, with four daughters, one in heaven, and eight grandchildren. I have awakened to the beauty of intentional intimacy with God, whose sole desire is to help men, women, and families to engage in intentional intimacy with God through a relationship with the Father, with the Son, and the Holy Spirit, as they grow in prayer, studying the Scripture, and sharing their faith.

ABOUT THE AUTHOR

EDDIE COX is an Ordained Pastor who ministers into the homeless populations in his hometown of Dallas Texas and throughout the United States and Internationally. Eddie has been on a journey of growing in authentic intentional intimacy with God since 1998. Please click on website link below and find out about Intentional Intimacy Ministries Mission statement and what we they are about, please be sure to check out the Empty Lot section and interact with us.

Website: http://intentionalintimacyministries.com